PRAISE FOR

DR. MICHAEL LARDON AND
FINDING YOUR ZONE

"Here is a guy who gets it. If you are interested in challenging yourself to greatness, this book will take you there. Michael has presented a great tool for learning how to compete with the best. He is among the best at growing peak performance."
—Flip Flippen, author of *New York Times* bestseller *The Flip Side*

"Dr. Lardon is the tool master. There are a million athletes who have the talent, the drive, and the ability to succeed, but unless you find someone to help you put those tools together, you can't do the work. Dr. Lardon helped me to believe in myself and to understand that no matter what happens, I have what it takes to overcome anything. And that's what I did. As long as I live, I will never be able to repay him for that gift."
—Jimmy Shea, Olympic gold medalist, skeleton

"Finally, truth you can trust! Dr. Lardon hits the bull's-eye with the essence of how we can achieve peak performance in all aspects of life. This is a fact book, not a fad book. In a world of hype, spin, and quick fixes, *Finding Your Zone* stands apart as an authentic guide to find the champion within."
—Denis Waitley, author of *The Psychology of Winning*; former chairman of psychology, U.S. Olympic Committee, Sports Medicine Council

"Dr. Lardon demystifies the intangible qualities of the 'Zone experience.' He illustrates how to remove the mental and emotional blocks that limit our abilities and couples it with a roadmap to those flow moments we've all had a glimpse of. His work is a wonderful blend of knowledge, experience, and wisdom, which are the right ingredients for both the athlete and the layperson to apply to all areas of life."
—Dr. Joe Dispenza, author of *Evolve Your Brain*; one of fourteen scientists featured in the multi-award-winning movie *What the Bleep Do We Know?*

continued . . .

"Doc Lardon helps me be me on the golf course. I'm an emotional guy and he has taught me how to move with my emotions and, if I have to vent, I vent. I slow down and look at the big picture, not focus solely on what's bad. He has also shown me that playing golf is not just about what happens on the course. Whatever is happening in my life is going to impact my game. It's important having Doc on my side."

—Rich Beem, 2002 PGA champion

"*Finding Your Zone* is not just a book on sports psychology; it is an educational and self-help book as well. What I love about this book is that Dr. Lardon not only explains 'the Zone' and how to get there, but he also explains many concepts and terms usually only known to members of the medical field. After reading this book, you can't help but be smarter and more well-rounded. And this isn't just about sports! His lessons can be directly related to everyday life and how to approach adversity from a position of strength."

—Tim Mickelson, University of San Diego, golf coach

"I started working with Dr. Lardon at the end of the worst season of my career. At the finals of the 2006 qualifying school I felt calm and relaxed and, more important, I enjoyed the six grueling rounds I played. I ended up with a PGA Tour card when twelve months earlier I had contemplated quitting the game. Working with Dr. Lardon has been invaluable." —Craig Lile, PGA Tour rookie

"As a young table-tennis player I always looked up to top players like Mike Lardon. These were the players I wanted to emulate. Now, as a two-time Olympian and coach working for the U.S. Olympic Committee, I can say with complete confidence that Dr. Lardon has summed up all the key elements to peak performance on demand. If you plan to 'go for the gold,' this is the book."

—Sean O'Neill, five-time U.S. men's single champion

"If you are looking for peak performance in sports, business, or life, *Finding Your Zone* is the roadmap."

—Dave Binn, NFL Pro Bowl long snapper, San Diego Chargers

"Dr. Mike literally can be credited with saving my career and enhancing my everyday life. He has combined his incredible knowledge of the mind and body to help me realize that the physical, psychological, spiritual, and professional are all linked. I cannot thank him enough. There is no other person in the field better than Dr. Michael Lardon."

—Michelle McGann, seven-time LPGA Tour winner

"At the highest level everyone has the talent but it is the mind that separates the good from the great. Dr. Lardon helped me during the most difficult time of my bobsled career when I was struggling to make the Olympic team. He helped me stay focused and believe in myself. I accelerated past my competitors making my first Olympic team in 2006 and winning the World Cup in 2007."

—Steve Holcomb, 2006 Olympian and 2007 World Cup champion, bobsled

"Dr. Lardon has helped me get my personal life under control so that I can better focus on my athletic goals. When I met him in March of 2007 I was emotionally at rock bottom, making my athletic future uncertain. He helped me get back on track to not only make the 2007 U.S. National Rowing Team, but also win the 2007 World Championships only six months later."

—Samantha Magee, 2004 Olympic silver medalist and
2007 World Champion, rowing

Ten Core Lessons
for Achieving Peak
Performance in
Sports and Life

FINDING YOUR
ZONE

Michael Lardon, M.D.

A PERIGEE BOOK

A PERIGEE BOOK
Published by the Penguin Group
Penguin Group (USA) Inc.
375 Hudson Street, New York, New York 10014, USA
Penguin Group (Canada), 90 Eglinton Avenue East, Suite 700, Toronto, Ontario M4P 2Y3, Canada
(a division of Pearson Penguin Canada Inc.)
Penguin Books Ltd., 80 Strand, London WC2R 0RL, England
Penguin Group Ireland, 25 St. Stephen's Green, Dublin 2, Ireland (a division of Penguin Books Ltd.)
Penguin Group (Australia), 250 Camberwell Road, Camberwell, Victoria 3124, Australia
(a division of Pearson Australia Group Pty. Ltd.)
Penguin Books India Pvt. Ltd., 11 Community Centre, Panchsheel Park, New Delhi—110 017, India
Penguin Group (NZ), 67 Apollo Drive, Rosedale, North Shore 0632, New Zealand
(a division of Pearson New Zealand Ltd.)
Penguin Books (South Africa) (Pty.) Ltd., 24 Sturdee Avenue, Rosebank, Johannesburg 2196, South Africa

Penguin Books Ltd., Registered Offices: 80 Strand, London WC2R 0RL, England

While the author has made every effort to provide accurate telephone numbers and Internet addresses at the time of publication, neither the publisher nor the author assumes any responsibility for errors, or for changes that occur after publication. Further, the publisher does not have any control over and does not assume any responsibility for author or third-party websites or their content.

Copyright © 2008 by Michael T. Lardon
Cover art and design by Elizabeth Sheehan
Text design by Ellen Cipriano

First edition: June 2008

Library of Congress Cataloging-in-Publication Data

Lardon, Michael.
  Finding your zone : ten core lessons for achieving peak performance in sports and life / Michael Lardon.—
1st ed.
    p.   cm.
  Includes index.
    ISBN-13: 978-0-399-53427-0 (Perigee trade pbk.)   1. Achievement motivation.   2. Performance.
3. Self-actualization (Psychology)   4. Success.   I. Title.
  BF503.L37 2008
  158.1—dc22   2008002557

PRINTED IN THE UNITED STATES OF AMERICA

10

Most Perigee books are available at special quantity discounts for bulk purchases for sales promotions, premiums, fund-raising, or educational use. Special books, or book excerpts, can also be created to fit specific needs. For details, write: Special Markets, Penguin Group (USA) Inc., 375 Hudson Street, New York, New York 10014.

*For my best friend and brother, Brad,
a gifted athlete who has both inspired and
motivated me throughout my career; and for
all the great athletes with whom I have had the honor
to know and the privilege to help.*

CONTENTS

Foreword by David Leadbetter   xi

Introduction   xiii

Lesson One   Dream   1

Lesson Two   Be Prepared to Overcome the Odds   15

Lesson Three   Transform Desire into Will   29

Lesson Four   Trust Your Brain, Keep It Simple, and
Stay Positive   47

Lesson Five   Stay in the Now and Be in the Process   65

Lesson Six   Manage Your Emotions and Thoughts   85

CONTENTS

Lesson Seven Keep Your Motivation Pure   103

Lesson Eight Acceptance and Faith Conquer Fear   121

Lesson Nine Build Confidence and Win   135

Lesson Ten Perform under Pressure   145

Acknowledgments   155

Index   157

FOREWORD

I have known Dr. Michael Lardon for a number of years. He has made a huge difference in my personal life. He is an experienced psychiatrist in sports issues and has competed professionally at the highest level. Mike can really relate to what it takes to perform at this level. As a golf coach I have had the opportunity to work with some of the game's greatest players including Nick Faldo, Nick Price, Ernie Els, and Greg Norman. I know that along with their great talent, they have something intangible that separates them from the rest. Dr. Lardon, through his scientific studies, research observations, and firsthand experience with all types of athletes, has come up with a no-nonsense, hardcore approach on how to move into the Holy Grail of the mental "zone."

Whether you are a professional athlete or a weekend warrior who would like to move up the mental ladder and improve your performance and quality of life, you will find this book a gem. I have seen firsthand how Doc Lardon, a caring and very humble human being, has changed people's lives through medicinal, psychological, or common-sense approaches, and I am excited that he is going to share his vast knowledge and experience here. They say the power of the mind is a vast untapped reservoir, and in the pursuit of excellence, Doc Lardon has the keys to help unlock the positive power of this reservoir.

—David Leadbetter

INTRODUCTION

Victory is for the one,
Even before the combat,
Who has no thought of himself,
Abiding in the no-mindness of Great Origin.
—D. T. SUZUKI, 1959

We are a nation that loves sports. We watch them on TV and play them at home and sometimes even at work. We play sports with intensity and joy. It is no surprise that we revere those athletes who rise above, like great stars shining brightly in the night sky. Superb athletes capture the essence of the human spirit and showcase human potential—they take huge risks, practice with unwavering dedication and commitment, and then put it all on the line, keeping us enthralled and mesmerized. We find ourselves vicariously sharing their innate human drive to self-actualize. We marvel at their power to perform under pressure, to stay focused on the present and play without distraction. It is the champion that learns to let go of control and worries—and trust his intuition and inner faith. He accepts the possibility of losing, and in so, paradoxically wins. This ability to perform under stress is essential for survival in sport as it is for all of us in life, and this is why sports are a wonderful encapsulation of life—an intensified microcosm of how we live. These are some of the reasons why athletes give us courage and inspiration and become role models for our daily lives.

Yet it remains a vital question why some athletes, with similar physical prowess and skills in relation to their peers, consistently seem to perform better under pressure. Tiger Woods's incredible curling chip shot in the final round of the 2005 Masters that clinched his victory seems to have been magically destined. Eric Heiden's win of five individual Olympic gold medals in 1980 was a display of absolute athletic genius on the world's biggest stage. Lance Armstrong's victory over cancer seemed to preordain his seven Tour de France titles. All of these athletes are champions in their respective sports, but most interestingly they have excelled in the sport of life. They have all achieved great heights in spite of great challenges. What makes them so different? And more important, how can we learn from these exceptional athletes and use this knowledge to help us in our daily lives?

WHAT IS THE ZONE?

The Zone is the ability to perform at your highest level in whatever domain of life. It is not a phenomenon exclusive to sports; it exists in every endeavor to which men and women apply themselves. But most people who achieve this higher consciousness and intense level of engagement get to this state of mind by accident. And this is why so many of us assume there's something magical about being in the Zone.

However, the Zone is not a magical state. It's also not something you can buy for $19.99 a month on the Internet. It's not something you can take a course to learn how to do. It is not achievable by taking medications, herbs, or by doing mind-altering hypnotic induction exercises. The Zone diet does not put you in the Zone. In fact, I have seen and heard innumerable claims by sports psychologists and others who declared they have scientifically developed ways to get into the Zone—and not one of these claims has ever panned out. I have even been told by a prominent sports psychologist who works on the PGA Tour and with National Hockey League (NHL) teams that he is a "performance enhancement expert" and he "removes emotional blockage that the athlete holds on to, enabling them to change at a cellular level and perform in the Zone at will." At first this sounded amazingly impressive to me, as were the number of athletes who believed him. In fact, I, too, wanted to believe him. So I asked him how he did what he did and he told me that it started with me giving him a three-thousand-dollar check. Alas, you can't pay for the Zone.

So why hasn't anyone debunked all this Zone stuff? Is it real or not? I am here to tell you that the Zone is indeed real; it's just much different than its popular misconceptions.

Through a lifetime of study, scientific research, and one-on-one work with athletes, I have repeatedly observed ten essential characteristics that the world's greatest athletes possess that not only enable them to perform at an optimal level but also allow them to transcend the distractions and everyday challenges that can potentially hinder their performance. Based on both my scientific research and personal experience, these components form both the basis of this book and the platform from which you can develop the mental acuity, the emotional power, and the skills that will help you improve your performance in whichever sphere of life you choose.

WHAT BROUGHT ME TO THE ZONE

Before I share with you these ten core lessons for finding your Zone, let me tell you a bit about myself and what brought me to understanding the Zone. As a teenager, I discovered table tennis, the second-largest participation sport in the world behind soccer. The sport suddenly "landed" in the United States by virtue of President's Nixon's famous invitation to the Chinese National Table Tennis Team to play against the American team at Madison Square Garden—"Ping-Pong diplomacy," as it was called. I began playing table tennis avidly, and by 1976, I was chosen by the U.S. Table Tennis Association (USTTA) as the most promising junior and awarded an eight-week trip to train in Japan with Nobuhiko Hasegawa and Shigeo Ito, the 1967 and 1969 world champions, respectively.

Over the next summer I lived at Senshu University in Tokyo and became entranced in watching a variety of sports that were also part of the university; in particular I loved watching the master martial artists train. Unlike any other athletes I had ever witnessed, these martial artists seemed to be training their minds as much as their bodies. I watched them break boards, bricks, and stones with their bare hands, their feet, and even sometimes with their heads—I was fascinated by the sheer physics of what I was observing. I soon realized that it was a transfer of energy that led to their mastery of these ancient sports. The Japanese martial artists concentrated so fiercely while they "shadowed" the blow they were about to deliver, and with one furious explosion, their arm, foot, or head would simply pass through whatever object they were breaking— like a hot knife through butter—and then it was over. I remember asking them how they do such a feat, and one responded, "You must leave no trace of yourself."

What was so fascinating for me was the realization that it was the mind that created the potential energy. The martial artists made repeated and quickening shadow motions prior to the actual strikes, mentally building an image of their hands passing through the objects. Once they reached a certain mental threshold, they released the blows, transforming the required potential energy into kinetic energy and exploding through the object. With mental focus and concentration, this potential energy was then transformed into physical movement. This was my first experience observing that optimal performance and the accompanying capacity for greatness begins with the mind.

Later that year, in December, the USTTA had the first U.S. Table Tennis Championships at Caesar's Palace in Las Vegas, Nevada. I was seeded twelfth in the juniors and didn't really know what to expect. I won several very close matches, and the next thing I knew I was in the finals against the perennial U.S. Junior Champion, Perry Schwartzberg.

The night before the match I was nervous, unable to sleep. I remember trying to quiet myself and relax by repeating a Zen mantra I had learned in Japan: "Victory is for the one who has no thought of himself before the combat." Later that night I started to dream of watching myself play the next day's finals as if I were watching a movie that was shot from a camera high above the table.

The dream was not like other dreams. It was so real that all my senses were hyperacute: Colors were more vivid, sounds were pure, and my touch was incredibly soft. I had a sense I could almost direct the dream while watching myself smash backhand and forehand shots alike. The experience of time felt nonlinear, and some shots almost looked like they were being played in reverse. I felt calm and quiet—like I was the sound engineer mixing music in a recording studio. Not surprisingly, I even saw myself easily winning—until I heard my 8:00 a.m. alarm clock start buzzing.

The next morning arrived and the crowd assembled. As the match began, I felt strange, as if I were living the dream of the night before. I started to warm up in front of the large crowd and heard their voices fade into nothing. Then I began to hear the emergence of a deafening silence juxtaposed with the sound of my racket grazing the ball. The Ping-Pong ball was slowing down, or at least that is what I thought. At speeds of up to 100 miles per hour, I still could see its direction of rotation, allowing me to block it, place it, and smash it at will.

Like the dream from the night before, I dominated the first two games without realizing what was going on. And then, when we were changing sides of the table, Tim Boggan, father of my two archrivals and friends, Scott and

Eric, said something like, "This is a huge upset." With those words, reality crashed in around me and I immediately fell out of my timeless time.

What happened? My meditation and dream of the night before had enabled me to walk into the arena the morning of my big match and access the Zone effortlessly. My play was at a higher level than I had ever accomplished before. And yet, as soon as I heard the words of Tim Boggan, who acted at times like my coach, I became conscious, and as such, separate from the moment of play. In short, I had been in the Zone, and then I fell out of the Zone. Perry won the next three games and the national championship.

Was I disappointed? Sure. But the bigger lesson was that I had experienced a piece of what I call "the timeless time." For me, table tennis became the vehicle that allowed access to the timeless time, a mysterious state of consciousness I had just visited and where all things seemed possible.

It was later, when I understood more about the Zone from both an intellectual and scientific point of view, that I wondered if the Zone, or what I began referring to as the timeless time, was something that happened when you did exceptionally well at work, or in school, or in art, or maybe even when you fell in love. I wondered if the Zone is a way we connect to God, perhaps allowing us to perform so divinely at times. But most of all, I realized that if my mind, like those of the martial artists, could create this energy that allowed me to perform outside of what I thought were my normal capabilities, others surely could do the same. All I needed was to find out who gets in the Zone, how they get into the Zone, and most important how they stay there.

A MISSION IS BORN: THE ZONE

I am now a medical doctor, specializing in psychiatry and the study of human behavior. I have specialized in sports and helping athletes for the last fifteen years, with most of my time focused on Olympians and professional golfers on the PGA Tour.

During my undergraduate training at Stanford University and my postdoctoral fellowship in psychobiology at the University of California, San Diego (UCSD) School of Medicine, I focused on the questions: Is there really an athletic "zone," a special state of mind that facilitates human peak performance? And if so, what are its biological, psychological, and spiritual underpinnings?

Throughout my fellowship at UCSD, I conducted extensive research at the Scripps Research Institute in La Jolla, California, with the help of Dr. John Polich, one of the world's leading brain wave specialists. Together we looked at the brain waves and various neuropsychological tests of some of the world's greatest athletes. The experiments were based on the idea or hypothesis that when great athletes get into the Zone, they are not bothered by all the extraneous concerns and worries that plague most of us in competition. For example, the San Diego Padres baseball Hall of Fame hitter Tony Gwynn did not worry about the people watching or hear the opposing team yelling "No batter, no batter" when he was trying to hit a 100-mile-an-hour fastball. In fact, on his best days, like the great Ted Williams would say, Tony probably saw the ball looking as big as a grapefruit with the rotation of the stitches giving away the type of pitch being thrown.

In our research we applied a very strong and specific scientific methodology by measuring a type of brain wave called event-related potentials, or ERP (ERPs measure how fast the brain processes stimuli). They have been used by the scientific community for more than fifty years to assess how well and quickly our brains process and respond to sensory stimuli and other information. Our studies applied this brain-imaging technology to elite athletes engaged in performance-related tasks or activities. The results suggested that Olympic-caliber athletes processed stimuli faster and earlier, allowing them to experience time as moving slower than nonathlete controls. They also produced greater amounts of slower (delta) brain wave activity, suggesting that they had more blood flow in critical parts of their brains.

What did this mean for both the elite-level athletes as

well as our average participants (i.e., our controls) in the study? It meant that the brains of the elite athletes worked more efficiently. Their brains responded better to the challenges at hand. Analogous to the difference between driving a big American car and a Porsche on a mountainous road, the brains of great athletes processed information and responded much more quickly than those of average people. However, to borrow a computer analogy, it was probably less about the hardware (the brain itself) and more about the software (their thought patterns).

This research was awarded grant funding approval in 1994 by the United States Tennis Association, was published in major scientific journals, and is unique for its assessment of high-performance athletes using advanced brain-functioning technology. The results of this research became the basis for the work I then began doing with athletes in both a clinical setting (i.e., in my office) and in real-life situations, where I began working one-on-one with athletes.

Throughout all of this research, as well as my years of clinical work with athletes, I have come to the conclusion that the Zone in its simplest form is a paradoxical state in which great physical feats are accomplished while the mind is empty and still, analogous to sitting in the cinema just waiting and watching for the movie to begin. It is a place where you can almost access an unlimited source of power and often realize your potential. Rosalyn Fairbanks, a professional tennis player, described for me two occasions where she beat both Monica Seles and Tracy Austin. She said she felt like she was "being controlled by a more powerful source—God," as she put it. On those days, "I felt superhuman; I was at another level of consciousness."

Interestingly, our research also showed that these athletes reported peak performance states outside of athletics, in their daily lives. Peter Vidmar, two-time gymnastic Olympic gold medalist, told us that he can get so absorbed in various tasks that his wife tells him that it takes a few moments before he can recognize his own children. Scott Tinley, triathlete and twice Ironman World Champion, described that when he plays guitar well, he feels the same timelessness that he feels during his best Ironman performances. Steve Scott, Olympian and one of the greatest milers in the history of track and field, spoke about feeling like he is in the Zone while playing video games—that things seemed "like he was in a bubble" of concentration. Brenda Taylor, the 2001 NCAA 400-meter hurdle champion, also described a "bubble of concentration" in which she felt protected from the camera clicks and screams of thousands of fans when she qualified for the 2004 Olympic team with one of fastest times ever recorded by an American. She said she could feel the power her hips and legs provided her as she flew over each hurdle. She even remembered how she felt her running shoe spikes tear the dirt with each stride. Brenda said she also felt the same way when giving lectures to large groups and most recently when she took her GMATs (business school entry exams) test. It is no surprise Brenda is starting her first semester at the Wharton School of Business, one of the world's best programs.

Simply put, the Zone is a mental state in which your thoughts and actions are occurring in complete synchronicity. The thinking part of the brain, the cerebral cortex, is bypassed and one's mind is actually operating at a more primitive, reflexive level while being fully engaged. When the thinking brain is quiet it can react (or act) more efficiently, sampling increments of time in smaller intervals, which is why people who have experienced the Zone talk about feeling as if time passed slowly and effortlessly. The 100-mile-an-hour baseball comes in slow motion; the feeling is calm and the result is often beyond expectation. Children playing are in the Zone. They do not have to have a magic drug or mantra. They don't need a $400-an-hour shrink. The Zone is not a magical place, although it feels that way. Indeed, it is a state of mind, an attitude, and a mental goal that all of us possess the potential to attain.

And though we are all born in the Zone, we spend most of our lives living distantly from it in a world of worries that we self-create. Sometimes trauma, loss, and love shock us back to this primordial place, but mostly we never find it—except by accident. The research we conducted at UCSD and Scripps Research Institute first suggested that there were four characteristics people experienced when they were in the Zone: (1) superconcentration, or complete mental absorption in a task; (2) the experience of time slowing down; (3) a sense of detachment from outside influences; and (4) a resulting supernormal performance. However, the more intriguing question became: Are there common thought and behavioral patterns great athletes exemplify that allow them to flow in and out of the Zone while performing? It is this question that gave rise to the ten common principles I have seen over and over again. These ten principles or core lessons are the substance of this book. Fortunately, through these ten lessons, the Zone is not only attainable by elite athletes, it is attainable by ordinary people like me and you. Indeed, the nonathletes, who were the controls in the same studies, reported that they had days at work and in their personal lives when "everything just went right"; when they "couldn't do anything wrong"; when they felt "connected to everything" they did; and when "things were effortless." We had a teacher tell of us of times when she taught her students that her lessons just came out of her "seamlessly, without notes, and the class would be mesmerized and not even rush to the door when the hour ended." We had a car salesman tell us that there were days he knew would be magical, and they resulted in closing the sale with all his potential customers. These people were not professional athletes, but they had clearly had a taste of the Zone. This phenomenon of the Zone generalizing outside of sports inspired me to look for a template, a prescription or framework, to help start regularly finding the Zone, in sport and, most important, in life.

Although we did find that some people, specifically high-level athletes, had a predisposition for the Zone, our research also demonstrated that it was not a genetically exclusive club, but rather a combination of multiple factors—most of which are based on very simple actions and decisions—that enable and set the stage for finding the Zone time and time again. So now, years later, by working backward from these results, coupled with my good fortune of having an unusually intimate vantage point to study these athletes, I have been able to isolate and distill what exactly made Eric Heiden different from other speed skaters; what made Lance Armstrong overcome a deadly illness in order to win seven Tour de France titles; what made one PGA golfer better than another, and what makes one businesswoman more successful than her peers.

Surprisingly enough, despite all the fancy science I've used in studying the Zone, I have found it is less about human physiology, and rather more about human determination and will. As a psychiatrist, I see this apparent paradox all the time: Medicines can help reverse or prevent some illnesses, but it is often the heart and soul of a person, those elements invisible and untouchable, that bring true healing. In working closely with all kinds of athletes, helping them to maximize their talents and learn to win under pressure, often I am simply helping them get out of their own way. When they learn to reduce their distractions, increase their focus, trust their innate talent, and access their will, they build confidence and often find the Zone—and win.

The Zone is within your grasp—it lies within your being and it is part of your human nature. But even though this almost mystical state of the Zone truly exists, it does not happen frequently by chance nor by hypnotic induction, but by following ten concepts that are universal among the world's greatest athletes. If you embrace and integrate these ten lessons into your life, you will learn to access the Zone. I've seen it happen time and again with many of the athletes and nonathletes I've had the privilege of helping. The secret is, there is no secret. There are simply ten things you must do.

LESSON ONE

DREAM

I dream of the dragonfly
who dreams of me.
—Anonymous

I love the above quote for two reasons. First, it suggests that you can dream of something, a goal, a psychic or physical entity, or a new reality, and by dreaming of it, you give it life. Second, it implies we are not separate from the world, but rather we are part of the world. Everything we do—even dream—helps shape the life we live.

As a scientist and doctor, I know that dreams are creations from our unconscious mind. When we awake and remember our dreams, we are remembering a vision created by our unconscious thoughts while our conscious mind was asleep. Sometimes we dream of what comes the next day. It may even be a big table tennis match, where for one brief moment we might experience the timeless quality of being in the Zone, dancing on the road to self-actualization. Sometimes our dreams are much simpler but just as effective: You dream that you go to the dry cleaner, and in the morning instead of forgetting this mundane task, you reflexively gather your laundry and deliver it to the cleaners.

Dreams can be squandered or they can be nurtured and grow into a force that participates in how we live our lives. But we also can have great dreams, and these have the power to manifest our desires, aspirations, and goals and bring them to life. When you become more aware of your dreams, hone them, even direct them, you begin to create a pathway to the Zone. For in essence, the Zone is a dreamlike state, a state in which the flow between the conscious and the unconscious mind is unencumbered. So if you are able to tap into your dreams, you begin to tap into the Zone.

MAKING DREAMS REAL

Dreams tell us stories about ourselves, about who we can be and what we can do. This use of dreams as a way of both hearing our stories and creating them is an art that can be cultivated and was epitomized by our Native American cultures, in particular the Hopi Indians. The Hopi Indians believed that their dreams had great meaning, and it was common for them to discuss them in detail in their daily lives. They thought of the dream world as a reality as valid as everyday life. Dreams were thought of as a higher level of being, an access road to the collective unconscious of all living things, and the Hopi invested tremendous mental energies in understanding and valuing these dreams. They are legendary in their use of dreams for prophesying about the future of mankind. In fact, in 1976 their influence even captured the attention of world leaders when their elders were asked to address the United Nations General Assembly in Vancouver, British Columbia, on the issue of world peace and mankind's future.

The beauty of dreams is that they are the product of our mind's power to process our life issues and desires without any conscious effort being put forth. All we have to do is give ourself a nighttime suggestion and remember in the morning to write down what we learned.

DREAM TO DISCOVER KNOWLEDGE

Dreams create unseen influence and can provide us with vital undiscovered knowledge. We spend approximately one-third of our life sleeping and dreaming in this paradoxical state of physical rest and vibrant mental activity, and we are largely blind to its existence. It is no surprise that our present-day Western culture of cell phones and constant distractions does not teach us the tremendous value of one of our most powerful innate strengths—learning to be conscious of our own dreams. In fact, when we daydream, we are often ridiculed, yet daydreaming is another form of visualization, a key tool for creating the potential for higher performance. Many of our most cherished scientists, inventors, and artists have come to their most important discoveries and creations by accessing—and directing—their dreams.

As an undergraduate student, I had the amazing opportunity to take a class from Dr. Jonas Salk, inventor of the polio vaccine. Dr. Salk gave a small seminar with only ten of us in the class. He spoke to us about how many of humankind's great discoveries and accomplishments have been products of dreams—of our unconscious mind. During the seminar, Dr. Salk told us a story of how Albert Einstein dreamed of his famous theory encompassing all of nature's laws—$e=mc^2$. Dr. Salk then gave another example of how the great scientist Friedrich Kekule dreamed of a ring with six hoops and three snakes swimming between these hoops. He explained that Kekule used this vision to develop the concept of shared electrons. This concept has allowed scientists to understand the basic nature of organic molecules. Both Drs. Einstein's and Kekule's discoveries have revolutionized the modern world as we know it.

Dr. Salk also shared his own personal experience of discovering the polio vaccine. At the time, polio was even more voracious and pandemic than AIDS is today. Dr. Salk recounted that as his study of the polio virus became more and more intense, he began to have recurring dreams about the virus, in which his perspective shifted from observer to subject. During one of his dreams he became aware that he was dreaming and, based on his experience of his previous dreams, he was able to manipulate his perspective from observer to the subject itself, the virus. He said that in this state of being the virus, he saw his own (the virus's) vulnerability. The next day in his lab, he developed the successful strategy for eradicating polio. Dr. Salk's experience of being consciously aware of dreaming while dreaming is called a "lucid dream." Lucid dreams, although rare, are the most powerful dreams. They foster creativity and even facilitate problem solving.

TRUSTING AND BELIEVING IN YOUR DREAMS

It was Dr. Salk who opened the gateway to my understanding of the importance and power of dreams. Since that time, I have seen again and again how our dreams tap into our unconscious mind—the seat of our souls—of our greatest wisdom. Ironically, if we dream too much or dream in the day, we are ridiculed for being a daydreamer. But to be the giant we dream, we must embrace our dreams and follow the vision they provide us.

I have witnessed this power to realize one's dreams, believe in your vision, and make it happen many times. One such opportunity was with the legendary tennis player John McEnroe. In 1993 on several occasions, I spent time with John, at his home in southern California and on the road in Seattle. We enjoyed talking about the mental aspects of sports, and, as you can imagine, I was particularly curious about how this amazing athlete's mind worked.

During an especially frank discussion, I asked him, "Did you ever know or anticipate that you were going to be the world's best tennis player?"

With a curious smile on his face, he said (to paraphrase), "I always dreamed of winning the U.S. Open—playing matches, pretending I was in the finals—long before my good friend Vitas (Gerulaitis) and I actually got there. I think I realized my potential most clearly when I was a junior at Wimbledon and I qualified for the men's single event and played Jimmy Connors in the semifinals. I lost the match in four close sets, but I learned three things: One, I could almost beat Jimmy Connors and I was eighteen years old; two, I was going to get better; and three, I would be able to beat him soon enough."

What I found most interesting was that Mac related his story without conceit, in a matter-of-fact tone that was straightforward, simple, and logical. He never compared his performance to his peers. In fact, he was extremely gracious in describing how great André Agassi's service return was, and the brilliant speed of Michael Chang's footwork. Mac never engaged in what I call "comparative mind distraction." Most people would not believe that realizing a dream of becoming the world's best tennis player could be that simple—however, simple does not mean easy: *To never surrender to self-doubt* is a formidable task, one that John personified. Candidly, John said, "Everyone has some self-doubt; I wouldn't want someone to think that if he or she had some self-doubt that they weren't going to make it—what is important is what you do with it." Then we talked about how a little self-doubt can provide the energy to train a little harder and keep your edge. It is clear that Mac sublimated this energy to fuel his immense drive to be the best. He was determined not to surrender and this determination propelled him from a top junior to world's number one player. Indeed, if Mac did not believe in his vision inspired by lifelong dreams, he would not have become the John McEnroe of legend.

Indeed, John's ability to trust and believe in his own vision is an expression of his dream to become a great champion: It was the *trust and the belief* in his dream that made him Zone-like as a competitor.

Often I have patients who discuss a problem or a life question that makes them anxious and perplexed. Their anxiety prevents them from listening to their heart and trusting their dreams. In one case I was treating a client who had grown up in a very strict and pragmatic family that encouraged her to get a practical degree like accounting or engineering. She was very smart and capable of accomplishing her parents' agenda and agreed with their logic of having a safe profession. Throughout therapy she was consistently torn between wanting to be a writer, yet simultaneously fearful of the lifestyle she thought would accompany the choice. She continually weighed the pros and cons and, like any good argument, there was always ample reason to justify either choice.

After many months, I encouraged her to take a new tack and not listen to her rational mind, but listen to her heart. We started this process by having her keep a dream journal and sharing the contents and associations with me in treatment. Her dream journal included both nighttime dreams and daydreams. After about one month, her unconscious drive to become a writer was clear and overwhelming. Everything in her dreams unequivocally pointed to her deepest desire to become a writer.

Within a short time, she made a huge choice and gave up the traditional track set forth by her parents. She was lamented by them, and her friends questioned the wisdom, or lack thereof, of her choice. And now, many years later, she is a very successful writer and content human being who has the immense satisfaction of knowing that she used her courage and drive to become what she loved most in order to live an authentic life.

This simple suggestion of asking clients to take a moment before going to bed and thinking of a question or important situation to dream about often leads to dreams that unmask hidden obstacles and clarify important issues. The amazing thing is that it happens all by itself without our effort outside of making the initial suggestion. We can dream anywhere, day or night. The critical element is that we stay attentive to this important natural phenomenon.

However, dreams not only inspire us to self-actualize, but also serve as a mechanism to balance life's anxieties with our deepest desires. For example, our writer overcame her parents' (and her own) fear of needing a "safe" profession when she finally allowed herself to trust her own reoccurring dream of becoming an author. Only she knew in her heart what was right for her, and trusting her dream gave her the courage to overcome her fears. Similarly, we all have the ability to follow a certain path, but the correct path for each of us is not something scripted by parents or cultural values—it is a sacred knowledge that lives deep within our soul and is often expressed through our unconscious in the form of recurring dreams. They can be thought of as the visible smoke that rises from the battleground of our psyche. This battle of survival between id (where our unconscious desires live), ego (the awareness of everyday life), and superego (our moral structure) is done in secret far away from our conscious awareness. This amazing autonomous process is part of the essential fabric of human life.

Our dreams provide the potential energy to make our realities transform into something greater. Over the years I have seen that by enhancing our access to our dreams, we are not only given the information, but also the power needed to learn to live our own authentic life. When we develop relationships with our dream life, we develop a relationship with something that is part of a deeper self, the place where our mind and soul unite. It is our dreams that give us our direction, our inspiration, and drive to self-actualize.

Self-actualization is the innate drive for higher values and purpose. Human beings are at first driven to meet their basic physiological needs like food, shelter, and procreation. After these needs have been met, we strive toward safety, intimacy, and respect. In Abraham Maslow's classic 1943 paper "A Theory of Human Motivation," he studied the lives of great people such as Albert Einstein, Jane Addams, and Eleanor Roosevelt. He developed the paradigm of a "hierarchy of needs" in which the concept of self-actualization is the ultimate goal and, in short, can be defined as reaching one's fullest potential. The characteristics of the fully self-actualized individual include embracing the realities of the world without denial, developing a system of morality that is fully internalized and independent of external authority, and using creativity, exploring your own limits, and realizing your own potential. When we are in the Zone, we are for at least that moment self-actualized. Dreams that germinate and become transformed provide the energy of a self-actualized life.

We all have this ability, an ability to access the most powerful supercomputer in the world: our own brain. So the question is, why don't we? We fear things we don't understand even if they are part of us, like our own dreams. We inherently don't trust things we don't understand, and we don't like things that require effort or bring discomfort or delayed gratification.

However, great accomplishments take effort, and by mobilizing a little force within ourselves, we can learn to recall our dreams and write then down. If we do this and free-associate to the themes recurring in our dreams, we will tap into a great reservoir of wisdom and strength.

ACCESS YOUR DREAMS: AN EXERCISE

Below I have listed some simple and time-efficient techniques that can help you develop the ability to access your dreams and even experience a lucid dream. If you can consistently follow these guidelines on a daily basis, you will experience more clarity, vision, and direction in your life.

- The first goal is to remember one dream every night. This starts with keeping a dream journal at your bedside, and the moment you awake, before moving and thinking about other things, write down all that you can remember about your dreams. Ask yourself, what was it I was dreaming about? Write down whatever you remember, no matter how fragmented it may be.

- Each night before going to bed, briefly go through your dream journal and prime yourself to remember your dreams, to dream about something in particular, or even become aware you are dreaming.

- Optional: If you are determined to lucid dream, you can take advantage that REM sleep (our predominant dream state) occurs in 90-minute intervals, so set an alarm clock at either 4.5, 6, or 7.5 hours after you go to bed. This practice should result in you waking during a dream state. Once you are awake, give yourself the suggestion that you want to have a lucid dream and allow yourself to fall back to sleep. Often this practice will result in the experience of feeling that you are in conscious control of your dream while you are dreaming, thus giving birth to a lucid dream.

- You should also use your journal to record your daydreams. Take your journal to a beautiful place and sit down, doing nothing except letting your mind wander. When your focus settles on an image, a thought, or an idea, sit with it, and let it give you direction and fuel your ambition to reach your highest goal.

If you can start by taking two weeks, and dedicate five minutes at night and in the morning to this, you will have started the process of becoming the giant you dream of being. Again, the most important task is to stay attentive to all of your dreams, day or night. Sometimes I wonder if indeed we create the dream, or if it is the dream that creates us.

BE PREPARED TO OVERCOME THE ODDS

Do not initially engage
a competitor unless
you are prepared.

—SUN TZU, *THE ART OF WAR*

The most common question I am asked by players on the PGA Tour is, "Doc, how is it possible that when I practice on the range I hit so pure, and on the course I hit so crooked? I am doing the same thing, yet when it counts I feel like I am a completely different person." The golfer is wrong. He is not a different person; a more accurate perception of what he experiences when he goes from the practice range to the competition is that he is faced with a different challenge. If he is still thinking about the swing-thoughts he used on the range, he will be blindsided by the unique challenges inherent in the competitive environment.

This phenomenon of being great in practice and markedly worse when it counts is not as inexplicable as it may seem. In Sun Tzu's masterpiece *The Art of War,* written over twenty-five hundred years ago, he said, "If officers are unaccustomed to rigorous drilling, they will be worried and hesitant in battle." The fundamental idea is that what happens in competition, in live theater, in the actual performance, cannot be replicated. There will always be unexpected challenges that arise that you cannot prepare for, that you cannot anticipate, and that will require you to think on your feet. If you are thinking about your swing during fierce competition, you've expended precious mental energy that will be needed when you are challenged with the unexpected. In the same way, if you are thinking about whether or not you completed a P&L statement during your presentation to your boss, you will undermine if not lose your focus and deliver a less-than-stellar report. Whether in sports, business, or life, if you do not adequately prepare before a performance, you do yourself a disservice: You keep yourself out of the Zone because the inherent pressure of the situation will usurp your energy and reveal your weak spots.

THE BEAUTY BEHIND THE CATNAP

In 2006, I was working at the Masters Golf Tournament in
Augusta, Georgia, and Phil Mickelson did something very
unusual. He was positioned to win the tournament on the
final day and, as is customary for a leader, scheduled to tee
off in the afternoon. What had really caught my attention
was not Phil's masterful performance, but rather that he
was napping just prior to teeing off. Most commonly, if
someone is about to go on to a huge stage and potentially
define his or her career, the anticipation and anxiety, no
matter how tired the person is, will not only keep him
awake, but compel him to practice up until the last second.
Think how many of us have stayed up all night studying
before a big test, reviewing notes until the last minute,
only to do poorly and not reflect the knowledge we possessed? Phil was different—he was on to something.

Counterintuitively, the great champions know not to
practice compulsively up until the last minute. They recognize that what they need most in these final hours before a
big showdown is to eliminate the clutter, the worry, and
create the clear frame of mind needed to deal with the fluid
and ever-challenging environment of competition.

Phil, with the help of his coaches Rick Smith and Dave
Peltz, had comprehensively prepared for the tournament
for weeks—working on his short game, his course

management, and most of all his driver. In fact, he had plotted out his game plan to such detail, he used two different drivers during the event, anticipating that each one would provide an advantage on certain holes. This level of detail is rare even on the world's biggest stages. He knew he was ready, and when he found himself a bit tired before the final round, he did not worry and panic; he did not get in any last-minute practice, but rather he rested and took a catnap while millions of people eagerly anticipated his performance. The result? Phil won.

Napping immediately before teeing off in the final round while holding the lead of the Masters seems very unusual for the average competitor, but the great athletes have the ability to know what it is they need to do, and do it regardless of circumstance. Phil was not overly anxious and what he needed was a little rest. Similarly, before competition, Jack Nicklaus would do what he needed to get ready and not more. When asked how much he would putt before a tournament, he would say that he would putt until he felt he was making a nice stroke and rolling the ball well, and after making a few putts he would put the putter in the bag and walk over to the tee.

The same method applies to arenas beyond sports. In business, the people who prepare systematically before a big presentation generally perform their best on the day of the presentation itself. The skill and knowledge that is required to perform well under pressure is not obtained moments before the performance. As with golf or any other sport, you have to be able to take your game from the driving range to the course: Comprehensive preparation takes foresight and is obtained over many weeks, months, or years of dedicated work. When you've accomplished this level of preparation, then your mind is more at ease during times of pressure or stress. Great preparation allows you to lose your worries and simply become one with the task at hand.

Recently, Craig Lile, a young South African golfer on the Nationwide Tour, came to me to help him master his anxiety and achieve the next level in golf. Despite being a very skilled golfer with a beautiful game, he had never played or had even seen a PGA Tour event. In our first few consultations, I observed his work ethic, diligence, and attention to detail. He often took notes about everything and clarified my suggestions. He was a dream client. Over the course of the year, he practiced, practiced, practiced, and ultimately went from #107 on the Nationwide Tour to #27. Because he wasn't in the top 20 and did not automatically qualifying for the PGA Tour, he was sent directly to one of the most terrifying experiences in professional sport, the finals of the PGA Tour Qualifying School.

I have had the opportunity to caddie for my brother, Brad, in several of these finals, and the experience is almost inhumane. I even saw a United States amateur champion on his knees crying in front of his wife and children after missing the cut. The Q School, as it is known, is so brutal because the golfer's record over the entire year means nothing. He often has to survive fourteen rounds of play (almost one thousand shots) without making any disastrous mistakes. If you make one bad swing you are often finished, and your next year can be spent teaching golf at the local driving range. However, if you make it through, you are set for the entire year. You have earned a PGA Tour card and can play each weekend for the $5-million-plus purses, not to mention the minimum of $300,000 in endorsement contracts. The swing is enormous and the pressure is palpable.

After the first day of the infamous Q School finals, Craig called me and said, "Dr. Lardon, it felt so strange today. I felt so prepared that I was hardly nervous." Six days later, after living in his own private bubble of calmness, Craig Lile became a PGA Tour rookie. He was able to deal with all the challenges presented by high-pressure competition and not worry about his swing. His preparation allowed his swing to be automated, and it was a great pleasure for me to see him in Hawaii this last year at the PGA Tour's Sony Open, make the cut, and receive a $25,000 paycheck in his first PGA Tour event.

AUTOPILOT

If you practice anything long enough, it becomes automated—solving math problems, giving sales pitches, even doing brain surgery are not exceptions. Performing at the highest level in competition always involves thinking on your feet. Any component of your performance that can be practiced can be automated. This ability to adapt and automate is the beauty of the human body and mind. We don't have to think about it—automation happens when we practice any task.

Let's take an example of a little league baseball player who finds himself anxious, struggling to hit because his peers throw the ball too fast. He can use his body's innate ability for adaptation to improve his hitting if he is willing to put in the extra effort and go to the batting range and place the pitching machine on a speed faster than what he is used to seeing. He might at first find himself anxious with the new challenge; however, his mind and body will inevitably allow him to acclimate to the faster speed. When he returns to his little league game and it is his turn to bat, he will find that the speed of the ball that previously intimidated him now invites him to smash it. As he continues to rise up in the ranks of competition, he may encounter a pitcher who throws a nasty curveball, a pitch he has never seen before. Because he is well prepared, he no longer wastes energy worrying about the speed of the pitch; he is not overwhelmed when faced with the novel challenge of hitting a curveball. He has a mental energy reserve that he can mobilize to deal with this new challenge. It is the extra practice coupled with his own innate ability that allows him to take his skill to the next level. This process of practicing and preparing allows the mind to perform tasks that initially require conscious awareness to become automated and executed at an unconscious level, conserving precious mental energy. Unequivocally, the best way to maximize your adaptability is simply to be comprehensively prepared.

Impeccable preparation makes anxiety manageable. It is helpful to realize that the moment you are placed in a competitive environment, whether a golf tournament or a presentation to your boss, some anxiety is inevitable. Competitive environments are anxiety-causing by nature. However, the silver lining is that a little anxiety is good. The associated natural adrenaline gives you increased focus and strength.

However, too much anxiety can be paralytic. It's this delicate balance of having just enough anxiety that allows you to perform optimally without letting the floodgates open. To illustrate this concept, let's look at the graph on the next page. On the y axis (vertical) we will plot the variable of performance level. The higher up you go on the y axis, the better the performance. On the x axis (horizontal), the farther right you move, the more anxiety you incur. However, in the middle section of the x axis exists the optimal anxiety, or optimal arousal state.

To further understand how you can take advantage of this relationship between anxiety and performance, imagine you are placed in the position of giving a big presenta-

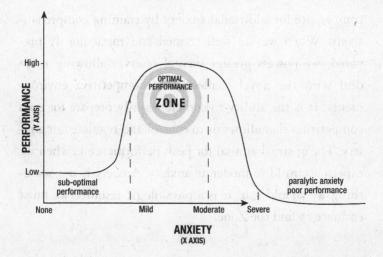

tion and you start the lecture without any anxiety or excitement. Without some level of arousal, you are at a disadvantage. You need some level of arousal or your presentation will be flat and you will not do your best.

If, on the other hand, you are consumed with anxiety and worry, you will not be able to think straight or react freely, and once again your performance will suffer. However, if you experience mild to moderate anxiety you benefit from physiologic hyper-arousal without compromising your ability to react intelligently in the heat of battle. This is the optimal arousal state for peak performance.

Almost all performance tasks have some anxiety associated with them. This is a reality and we need to accept it. Furthermore, the moment the task is done in a competitive environment, the experience of anxiety increases. We can compensate for additional anxiety by training comprehensively. When we are well trained and meticulously prepared, we possess greater mental reserves allowing us to deal with the novel challenges of competitive environments. It is the ability to conscientiously prepare for each competition that allows us to control and regulate our anxiety. The optimal arousal for peak performance is when we experience mild to moderate anxiety. Anxiety is not something we should fear; it is a physiologic resource we must embrace to find the Zone.

ARE YOU TRAINED?

Preparation is not only essentially in sports. In the movie *Man on Fire,* Denzel Washington plays an ex-military, functioning alcoholic making his way back into society, working as a high-end private bodyguard for a wealthy family. At one point in the movie, he says, "Either you are trained, or you are untrained," implying that there is no middle ground for greatness. But greatness can mean so many things: proficiency, distinction, magnanimity, heroism, and superiority—all of these qualities are what characterize the Zone.

I like to think of "great" meaning the exploration and realization of your own potential. If we self-actualize, we then become great. But without total preparation, without being completely fully trained, as Sun Tzu once again tells us, we should not "engage the competitor." So, when I work with my athletes, I like to ask them the question, "Are you trained?" If they cannot quickly and affirmatively answer yes, I know we have work to do.

Imagine a strong, overly confident, competent skier invited to helicopter ski for the first time with some friends on a remote mountain. Throughout the ride he boasts about his competence and physical training. However, shortly into the trip he experiences shortness of breath and realizes that he is not fully acclimated to the altitude. He then hears and soon sees an avalanche come thundering close to his location. Suddenly he realizes that he is ill prepared. His ability to think is frozen by the overwhelming anxiety of experiencing an event that he had not properly anticipated, prepared for, or researched. His lack of preparation puts his life at risk. In the world of helicopter skiing, he is untrained. He does not know the nature of what he is doing. He has not taken time and effort to do the necessary research and concomitant preparation, to be well trained. His arrogance and lack of knowledge have blinded him from what it really takes to be fully prepared to re-create at the level of a competent helicopter skier. To be well trained, he must make it his business to prepare for what is likely to happen and what is unlikely to happen.

Jonas Salk did not accidentally discover the polio vaccine—he spent a lifetime creating the stage for his discovery. Phil Mickelson didn't just get hot and win the Masters one weekend—he started with mirroring his father's swing at two years old. If you want to take it to the next level in whatever pursuit, you must constantly ask yourself: How can I prepare? How can I prepare to be better? Who knows more than I do, and how can I learn from them? You must be careful not to let confidence mutate into arrogance because it will blind you from having the curiosity essential for learning. Knowledge is power, and preparation gives us a greater knowledge on how we will react in battle.

By constantly asking yourself "How well am I trained?," you will not fall into the trap of arrogance and laziness— you will stay on top of your game. Procrastination is incompatible with the athlete who thinks in these terms.

PREPARATION IS A BUILDING BLOCK

Preparation is the fundamental building block for maximizing performance and getting in the Zone. Forethought, planning, and rigorous training are essential, so when the bell rings you have no worries, only the excitement of meeting the unique and novel challenges of competition. Come the day of performance, you will know that you are well trained and there is no need to play catch-up. You will have the luxury of being in the moment and reacting to whatever your needs may be—even if it is taking a little catnap before teeing off in front of millions of scrutinizing golf fans.

In order to get in the Zone, you need the whole package: You have to have already practiced relentlessly for countless hours automating your body's movements and creating muscle memory, so that by the time you perform, you are not thinking; your body is thinking for you. If winning the medal or the tournament is your goal, then you need to be calm, rested, and relaxed. How do you accomplish such peace at a time when the tension naturally runs so high? Start by asking yourself one critical question: "Am I fully trained? Am I fully prepared?" Always keep in mind that great preparation happens long before the performance.

TRANSFORM
DESIRE
INTO WILL

The first step to becoming
is to will it.

—MOTHER TERESA

Most of us, especially those with our eye on the Zone of life, aspire to create or master something during our lifetime. Sometimes this desire to create or achieve is very specific: "I want to be an artist" or "I want to be a doctor" or "I want to travel the world" or "I want to be a wife and mother." Sometimes this life desire is equally as strong, but it takes a more general form: the desire to be the best we can be. This drive to discover our limits, indeed to push and maximize those limits, is embedded in the process of self-actualization. But unless we transform our desire into will, we not only cannot find the Zone of life, we cannot achieve self-actualization.

HOW TO DEFINE DESIRE

Many of us work endlessly trying to achieve our goals and satiate our desires. However, all too often our optimism and hope decay into feelings of confusion and disappointment. In this way, desire can be dangerous. In Buddhism it is taught that our attachment to desire is what leads to our own suffering. Nevertheless, desire is inextricably woven into the human condition. It is an essential energy that exists in the pursuit of realizing one's own life dream. However, only when this energy of *desire* is strengthened and transformed into the energy of *will* can your goal—whatever it is—be achieved fully and at the highest level, and this is the very nature of the Zone.

All too often desire is a wasted energy without direction or goals attached. In contrast, the energy of will is woven into the fabric of its goal. To further understand this concept, let us imagine a young boy waking up early in the morning in a big, cold house. As the alarm goes off, he snuggles, feeling cozy and warm under the safety of his blankets, knowing that soon he will be challenged by a moment of truth in which he must throw off the covers, walk through the freezing house, go to the shower, endure the cold until the warm water comes, and begin the day. It is in that moment, when the boy throws off the covers without hesitation, that he exercises his own will. But how does the boy manifest his will? How does this process occur?

William James, the father of modern psychology, gave a series of lectures at Harvard University (*Talks to the Teachers*, 1892) that can lend light to understanding this question. In his talk, Dr. James gave a similar example and posits that, in that moment when the boy is still in bed, he experiences two predominant thoughts: (1) enjoying the warmth under his covers, and (2) fearing the frigid air around him. These thoughts oscillate in a deadlock of hesitation and procrastination. The boy has only two choices that allow him to resolve the deadlock. He must either: (1) forget the warmth of the bed and the cold that envelops it and just get up and go; or (2) continue to be mindful of the need to get up and endure the cold, leaving him in a continual state of conflict and perturbation that can only be resolved by the same act of starting his day. In both cases, the boy throws off his covers and exercises his will. The underlying principle, in either example, is that his desire becomes coupled with his goal—bounded together as one, he is left with no choice but starting his day. Will is forged when the energy of desire is never released from its goal.

JUST PUT THE HAMMER DOWN

Speed skater Eric Heiden embodies the power of will beautifully. Eric was my lab partner in premed chemistry during college. One day he casually told me that he planned to compete in the Tour de France. I asked him if he was kidding. He was a premed at Stanford University, which had its own demands, and Palo Alto, California, was a long way from France—not to mention he was not a world-class cyclist. Typically, I would not doubt one of the most decorated Olympic champions of all time, but I found this plan "a little too pie in the sky" for even the famously gifted and modest Eric Heiden. Then he earnestly and logically explained to me, using a quasi-mathematical equation, that his legs could generate so many watts of power and that if he were to factor in his size and weight, he could make a bicycle accelerate and maintain a speed that translated into what was required for the Tour. He then shared that he had harbored this dream to race in the Tour de France for many years. When we talked about this or our shared goal of becoming doctors, he would use the phrase "Just put the hammer down."

At first I was unclear what he meant, but as time progressed I realized that he did not think like the rest of us. If he saw a path and felt that the essential variables were within his control, he never doubted his ability to achieve.

He judged himself only on his effort and not on the praise of others. Like John McEnroe, Eric instinctively avoided the all-too-common pitfall of engaging in comparative mind. He skated for himself and not others. He knew that *when* he put his mind to the task at hand, not *if* he did, he would reach his goal. His phrase "just put the hammer down" symbolized the melding of action and desire in order to forge will.

Throughout those college years, Eric trained on his bicycle between attending classes and studying. And sure enough, after graduation Eric won the United States Professional Cycling Championship and the next year competed in the Tour de France. The key to Eric's success, and what for me was most fascinating, was that he never related to his wish to cycle in the Tour de France as a desire. By the time he began training, his desire had already taken another form: Its energy was already attached to its goal. It had become, in essence, the potent and penetrating energy of will.

Another powerful example showing that everyone, or at least every woman, has the capacity of exercising will is the experience of childbirth. When women go into labor, their bodies are seized by pain and contractions; however, the focus of the experience never deviates from the goal of giving birth. They may scream or even cry and yell out in anger, but they never give up. Their ability to stay completely committed and focused on the goal gives them the strength needed to endure the grueling process and push the child into the world. This is also an exercise of will.

EXERCISING WILL

For many of us, the process of mobilizing our will is not easy. One of the most common impediments is that we romanticize the goals we seek, only seeing the end and not the whole process. We do not ask the questions: What is it we truly covet? What is the nature of what we seek? Is it the lifestyle of the rock star, the professional athlete, or the CEO of a *Fortune* 500 company we imagine? Do we conveniently forget about the relentless training, perseverance, work, and even occasional humiliation that can be part of the process of achieving greatness? Maybe, you will find out that deep down inside, you do not want to invest the energy required. If you see this, you have saved yourself tremendous energy and angst.

Let's take a hypothetical example: If you want to become a teacher, you must thoroughly research what courses are required to obtain the teaching credential. You must ask yourself if the goal is attainable, given your skills, your determination, and your ability to commit to the required course of action. You must ask yourself if you have the time, the financial means, the intellectual acumen, and the desire to match. You must honestly assess if it is possible. And if you thoroughly map out the necessary course and see that it is possible, then you are halfway there. You must be prepared to take responsibility to do the grunt work and endure the journey of your dream, or your desire will languish. But if you fuel your determination with unwavering commitment, without ambivalence, and make a decision to act on your desire—whether that be waking at 5:00 a.m. to swim laps, or staying up every night until 10:00 p.m. to practice the cello—then you match action to desire and thus create your most powerful ally: will.

Sometimes you may find that you need to do something that is necessary for your own survival, whether it be in sports or life, and you are unable to mobilize the energy needed. However, if you place yourself in an environment that reinforces the goal you are trying to achieve, you will often be successful.

George was a client of mine who was struggling with severe depression. His depression stemmed from his fifteen-year destructive affair with crystal methamphetamine. He miraculously had been able to maintain his sobriety for over a year, but the damage left by his addiction appeared irreparable.

Crystal meth, as it is called, causes a massive release of the neurotransmitter dopamine in the brain, which in turn creates a euphoria and tenacious self-reinforcing cycle of euphoric intoxication and dysphoric (unpleasant) withdrawal. After people have abused the drug extensively, they are unable to enjoy the simple pleasures of life. Watching your child hit a home run in little league normally causes the release of dopamine in your brain, but when your brain is depleted of this mood chemical, there is no feeling of happiness. Dopamine is released in the pleasure centers of our brain when we fall in love. Dopamine provides the natural high we all search for. A brain without the capacity to release dopamine is a formidable opponent for the patient and psychiatrist alike. George had this problem and he knew it. He told me he always felt that he was ready to relapse and that he was losing the will to live. All the medicines we used were largely ineffective.

George began to miss his appointments. At this point I took a firm stand and told him, "You can die or you can live—you have the choice. If you want to live, you must take responsibility for your life and fully commit to seeing me in treatment, or move on." Insolent with my answer, he demanded to know what it was I wanted. I said, "You must simply not give up." After an emotional silence, he nodded and agreed, and we moved on to a new phase in his treatment.

I encouraged him to free-associate in therapy and write down his dreams in a journal. George first talked about the happiest days in his life before his addiction and depression. He talked about his freshman math teacher and how much he liked him and the class. He went on to say that he had always wanted to become a teacher, and talking about his dreams only strengthened his desire.

The focus of our treatment moved from medicine to exploring the power within his unconscious mind. Over the months, we talked about every conceivable aspect of the courses required to obtain a teaching credential, including which ones would be hard and which ones would be easy. These discussions opened his eyes to the possibility of a new life, and it was in these times that I saw his depression show signs of weakness.

I encouraged George to do homework assignments that included outlining every requirement he needed from point A to Z to become a teacher. When I asked him to commit himself to all of this, he said I was asking too much. He was upset, stating that I was unrealistic and insensitive to the severity of his condition. I apologized and reiterated that all I asked was that he not give up. I then reframed the question and asked him to imagine that he would do all that he needed in order to achieve his dream of becoming a teacher and to imagine that nothing would stop him. He acquiesced with a sly smile, knowing that I was trying to trick him with my "pretend" concept.

We plodded on and our therapy continued. After several more months of recording both his day and nighttime dreams, plotting his course, and talking about what it would be like to teach high school kids, and in particular math, his mood brightened, but paradoxically he seemed caught in a state of conflict. Like the boy in bed, he had only one choice to resolve his conflict of indefinitely wallowing in his depression while longing for his goal. The next week he came in and told me that the day after our last session, he enrolled in several classes at the local community college and even talked to the professors about his struggles with depression and his dream to become a teacher.

It was then that I realized George had matched action with his desire. He continued his pursuit and soon passed his first-semester courses and started to gain momentum and take on more courses. His energy was coming back, and during one memorable therapy session he asked how was it possible to feel better if the crystal meth had burned out the dopamine system in his brain. It was a valid question, and I explained that scientifically I did not have a good answer except to say that I thought he had accessed a power stronger than his addiction or depression by nurturing his dream and acting on his desire. "And what on earth, Doctor, is that power?" he asked, and I replied, "Will."

Today, George teaches high school math for a private school in San Diego County.

GETTING BEYOND THE DISCOMFORT

So, what tools can you use to transform desire into will? The good news is that your mind is already equipped. If your friend blows a whistle in front of you and you cannot hear it, you are likely to think that the whistle does not work. Your experience of reality is that there is no whistle blown. If, however, you see a nearby dog become very agitated, you might reassess your reality and assume that your friend is blowing a dog whistle. The sound produced by a dog whistle is in a frequency range that we are physically unable to hear.

Just because we cannot hear the sound when the dog whistle is blown doesn't mean the sound isn't real. If a tree falls in the forest and no one hears it fall, it doesn't mean the tree didn't fall. And yet, it is inherently human to give reality only to things we can see, hear, smell, taste, or touch, which brings me to the concept of solipsism.

SOLIPSISM

Solipsism is the psychological theory that states that reality exists only within one's mind. Our minds, when under severe stress, have the capacity to filter out stimuli and modify our realities, which in turn allows us to adapt better to the situation at hand. An example is to imagine a soldier who loses a leg in battle and realizes he has to tie a tourniquet around his bleeding leg so he can survive. Later he reports that during the acute event he did not feel any pain. This happens because his mind automatically turned off the sensation of pain to prevent overwhelming anxiety that could disrupt his own ability to function. This is a survival mechanism that human beings have developed through evolution.

When our conscious mind has too many demands made on it, like dealing with severe pain while simultaneously having to tie a tourniquet around a bleeding leg for survival, our mind automatically dissociates (that is, removes itself from conscious awareness) one need so it can focus unhampered while attending to the demands of the other. Studies show that more than 60 percent of people have reported some dissociative experiences in their lives. It is our mind that gives reality its form. We can take advantage of this proclivity of the mind when we endure something difficult.

A personal example of this phenomenon is from my college days when my buddy Eric called me one day and asked me to go bike riding with him and his close friend Tracy. Excited to go and eager to impress the prettiest girl in the dorm, I asked Eric if I could bring a friend. Soon thereafter Georgia and I arrived at Eric's house, and he graciously built us both bikes from his fleet of frames and components. His friend Tracy was a good rider, however Georgia and I were not. We rode from the back side of the mountain down to the ocean, and for the first eighteen miles it was literally a breeze. When we reached the Pacific Ocean, we had a nice lunch and I soon realized that we had to ride home—a daunting task. After a few miles all uphill, Georgia became a bit upset and asked Eric if there was a shorter way home. He said that if we took the next right turn it would only be eight miles to his house rather than the fourteen miles in front of us. I looked at Eric, thinking, this does not make sense—what in the world are we doing? However, Georgia was happy with the shorter alternative and off we went.

After about twenty minutes of climbing this deserted mountain road, off limits to cars because of its steep pitch, Georgia started to cry and say some bad things about Eric and me. Angrily, I called Eric to come back, and we privately conferenced while I urged him to get us out of this mess. He calmly pulled out an extra tire tube, linked it from his seat to Georgia's handlebars, asked her to jump on, and started towing her straight up the mountain. Mesmerized, I watched his massive legs pump like giant pistons and later heard Georgia giggling and thanking him for such a fun day. Shortly thereafter we passed a young couple who had obviously made a wrong turn only to also find themselves in agony on this ridiculous road. I remember the wife saying to her husband, "Honey, can you please start towing me up the hill like that man?"—not knowing that "that man" possessed thirty-two-inch thighs and was Eric Heiden.

Before long I started to suffer terribly. As I fell behind the pack, I started to ruminate about the pain, about giving up and quitting, even wondering if I could die from heat exhaustion. Fortunately, forty-five minutes of torture later, my male ego got the best of me and I simply decided that I was not going to quit on my first ride with Eric and, even more important, I was not going to let Georgia think I was a wimp. Suddenly my mind stilled and I noticed everything about the rhythm of the climb. By keeping my attention on the rhythm of my stride, I found the strength to keep my focus by becoming single-minded and somehow I stopped noticing the pain. Did this mean that the pain stopped existing, or that I stopped giving it reality? I later learned that what I did unconsciously was to *solipsize* the pain.

Almost two hours later, I realized that I had been riding alone and my friends were long gone, but finally I saw the end of the mountain roads. I will never forget what happened next. Eric came driving down the hill on an obvious rescue mission. Upon seeing me, he stopped his truck and gave me a look like, "What's up? What's your problem?"

I glared back at him with indignation, thinking the problem was obvious.

"It's only a bike ride," Eric said, chuckling.

And in that moment I realized that for him it was only a bike ride. On the way back to his house, he went on to explain to me why pain was no big deal. He said pain is simply the result of nerve fibers carrying information to the sensory cortex of the brain, telling the brain that the muscles being used are stretching their limits. He punctuated this information with "and that's a good thing."

He went on to tell me that in his younger days, in the

summers in Wisconsin, he used to sit in the family Oldsmobile and close the windows and turn up the heat to see how much he could take. At another time, he told me, his mother actually caught him placing a hot steel linked chain on his bare legs in one of his "heat out" sessions. "She was real upset," Eric explained with a grin on his face. "She wanted me to see a psychiatrist."

Eric played with pain. He did not associate with fear and anxiety the way most of us do. His heat out sessions were done by design. In the cold Wisconsin winter, his speed-skating workouts demanded tremendous ability to endure the cold. During the coldest times, when all the other skaters had retreated to the warmth of the indoors, Eric created the warmth within his mind. He would remember how hot it had been in the Oldsmobile and re-create this reality so he could continue training. Eric instinctively understood that reality is all within one's own mind, and he often chose to attend to the reality he wanted and ignore the realities he did not. This is the art of solipsism at its highest level.

GOING BEYOND PAIN

The tool of solipsism is something everyone has the innate capacity to utilize; however, to access and strengthen this vital skill takes practice and effort. An easy exercise is to take a simple task that you really do not like to do; for the sake of argument, let's say it is doing the dishes. Before starting the exercise, you must make a committed decision that you will not get all worked up about who is going to do the dishes and why you don't want to, but let yourself go ahead and do them, as if, without thinking, you are on autopilot. Like the example of our boy throwing the covers off to start the day, go directly over to the sink and put on the dish gloves and start cleaning. Before you know it, the dishes are done and you may even come to find that, surprisingly, the task was not as hard as you anticipated. You will find that you have just increased your capacity to do something you do not like.

Try this same process and apply it to working out on the elliptical machine at the gym, and again you will be surprised at the result. Manage your own reality, and life will be easier. Keep practicing this type of exercise on tasks or projects that you don't like, and you'll find that as you are exercising your body, you are strengthening your will.

Desire is transformed into will through a process that first starts with practicing the exercise of engaging in tasks that are mentally difficult. These tasks may vary depending on the individual. They may be doing the dishes, reviewing spreadsheets, working out on the elliptical trainer, or practicing public speaking. The key is, the task must be mentally difficult for you. The goal is to transition your mind into a state of autopilot and learn to pass through the task without mental anguish. The more you practice and trust your ability to go beyond pain, discomfort, the more you enable yourself to functi dom, and access the Zone. Remember, the Zone by magic: It is the training of your mind that enables you to get there.

The next step is to choose your target—your goal. Study everything about your goal. What does it take to get there? What investment do you have to make? What is the nature of what you covet? Write everything down on a list and ask yourself: Do I have the necessary skill, the time, the resources, and lastly the desire and drive to complete the task? If in the final assessment, in your heart, you know that you can do all that you outlined, you just have created the mental stage of transformation. You are now mindful of both your desire and your path. It is only your inaction that creates conflict.

If you do not immediately act on your desire, you are procrastinating, but be patient and continually review your plan and your goal. Tenaciously hold on to your goal and do not release it from your heart. You may find that your thoughts are in a state of conflict, deadlocked in oscillation between inaction and the desire to reach your goal. Your internal conflict can only be resolved in one way. Like the boy, you must throw off the covers and start the day—you must match action with desire by following the plan you conceived. When you do this, the process is now engaged, and your desire has been forged into will.

TRUST YOUR BRAIN, KEEP IT SIMPLE, AND STAY POSITIVE

Those who think do not know.
Those who know do not think.

—ANONYMOUS

Threhe human brain is smart. It's smarter than the smartest supercomputer in the world. Developed over hundreds of thousands of years of evolution, our brain is able to pick up all sorts of information and stimuli, measure and make sense of the data, and even act on it—and all this happens without our conscious awareness. This incredible innate ability we all possess brings forth the possibility that maybe it is better in the midst of a competition to simply trust our instincts and not overthink the situation. This activity is different from preparation—mental or physical. Learning how to keep things simple follows the preparation. In other words, if you've prepared, it's now time to simply focus on what's in front of you and commit to the execution—of the shot, the deal, the task directly ahead.

KEEP IT SIMPLE

Several years ago I was asked to lunch by Dr. Sian Belock, a professor of psychology at the University of Chicago, who wanted to collaborate with me on a study looking at the relationship between how much time highly skilled golfers take before each shot (preshot routine) and their performance in pressure-packed situations. During our lunch she proposed that we do a collaborative project and study professional golfers at the 2004 Ryder Cup that year at Oakland Hills Country Club in Michigan. Her hypothesis was simple: She wanted to show that when highly skilled golfers take more time and overthink well-practiced routines in pressure situations, they throw their timing off and choke. In other words, don't overthink and keep it simple, and you will perform your best.

That year, the logistics of timing the players' preshot routines in the midst of the large crowds at the Ryder Cup made the study not feasible. But Dr. Belock's hypothesis lingered in my mind throughout the year. I could not help but notice that players often altered the time they took to prepare and hit shots in pressure-packed situations. When they took more time and "overthought" the shot, they did not perform as well. Similarly, when they rushed the shot, their performance also suffered. It was no surprise that when I brought a stopwatch to the 2004 Accenture Match Play Championship in Carlsbad, California, I noticed that Tiger's routine never changed. He always took the same amount of time with each shot, regardless of its importance. He provided more evidence to support Dr. Belock's hypothesis: Have a simple and consistent routine and you will find yourself in the winner's circle.

Similarly, Sam (Samantha) Magee, a member of the woman's two-thousand-meter crew Olympic team, told me that when they lost the gold medal race in Athens, they had felt distracted by all the media hype and pressure around the event. However, at the 2007 world championships in Munich, Germany, Sam and her teammates kept it simple and found the Zone. Sam said they had been humbled by the loss in Athens and learned to pay little attention to the hype before going into the final race. They all decided to focus on a very simple plan of "laying back for the first thousand meters, then making a hard move toward the finish." Sam said they did not care about the other teams' performance, only about executing their game plan and staying positively focused. Sam reported that when they reached the thousand-meter mark and started picking up the pace, the whole team did not feel pain—not the excruciating pain normally felt in the last thousand meters of this type of race, but no pain at all. They found themselves functioning as one unit, working in complete synchronicity and blazing to victory and a world championship. Through the team's choice of focusing on the execution of a simple plan, they prevented themselves from overthinking and getting in their own way.

JUST DOING IT

The success of Nike's slogan "Just do it" is not an accident—the slogan implies that by "just doing it," you get out of your own way so you can do your best—at whatever activity. The neuroscientist interprets this slogan to mean, don't let your conscious awareness get in the way of what your brain already knows what to do. When you have practiced comprehensively, your brain automatically ingrains patterns into its own neural circuits that become "preferential pathways." We create our own disruption of these brain pathways when we think too much, which leads to choking. In other words, you have to make a conscious effort to get off track or get in your own way to derail a very natural process. This is most commonly done with negative and extraneous thoughts. If we realize that our own brain is an amazingly competent biologic machine that has been forged through millions of years of evolution, then maybe we can allow ourselves the latitude to sit back, stop worrying, and watch it do its thing.

THE DELICATE BALANCE BETWEEN
EFFORT AND TRUST

An example of our brain's power is demonstrated by a famous study in 1897 by Dr. G. Stratton. Dr. Stratton utilized what he called "displacement goggles" that allowed the user to experience the world as if it were inverted. When he looked through these goggles, he saw the floor and his feet optically displaced up where the ceiling would normally be. He saw the ceiling down below him in place of the floor. In his diary he is quoted as saying that when he wore the goggles, his own arms and legs became optically displaced and that he felt "[his] limbs begin to actually feel in the place where the new visual perception reported them to be." In other words, his brain began to adapt to the new information of seeing everything upside down, which in turn allowed him to explore his upside-down world as right side up. This all happened without conscious awareness.

The idea here is that if we put on Dr. Stratton's optical displacement goggles, the floor would be seen where the ceiling is and the ceiling would be seen where the floor is.

At first, you would become disoriented. But after some time, only a day or so, your brain would adapt to your perception and the world would be perceived normally again. You adapt to the goggles without knowing it. You may be wondering what happens when you take the glasses off. At first, you become disoriented but after the same amount of time, your brain corrects your perception and once again things normalize. You do not have to consciously do anything except trust your own mind.

Our brain possesses these incredible abilities of which we are not aware. However, when we consciously try to control our performances, we unwittingly lose touch with—or undermine—our natural ability to adapt and perform in highly competitive environments. How can we learn to manage intense stress so that our brain is free to do its thing? It's a delicate balance between conscious effort and innate reflexive trust.

Often during tournament competition, professional golfers stress out, pressing to make birdies so they can make the cut and play on the weekend, but in doing so they ever so subtly change the rhythm of their swing and the timing of their preshot routine. They stop doing what they already know how to do and unknowingly start a destructive self-perpetuating cycle. This phenomenon of stressing out prior to and during performance happens in all domains of life, even in the competitive world of business.

It is human nature to react to stressful situations by feeling the need to do something extra, but it is this something extra that leads us away from what we need. We simply need to trust our own innate ability. To paraphrase Shunryu Suzuki from his classic text *Zen Mind, Beginner's Mind*, it is when you think you attain something special that you don't. However, when you give up no longer wanting something special, you do something special. It is the over-trying that impedes the realization of our ability.

For example, amateur golfers often focus their hopes on breaking through a particular threshold, let's say shooting 90 or below for eighteen holes. As they come close to their goal, they start to try even harder and press, which in turn inevitably results in hitting poor shots. When they realize that they cannot mathematically reach their goal, they become forced to accept the reality and finally relax, with the paradoxical feeling that they have just given up. It is in this moment, when they think they gave up, that they start trusting their innate ability and hit good shots again. This is because their subconscious is no longer preoccupied with the score. There is no splitting of attentional focus. When they give up and trust their natural ability, they engage in what the great Zen masters call "direct experience." This is another example of the delicate balance between conscious effort and innate reflexive trust that must exist to allow you to get into the Zone.

HOMEWORK

Three years ago I was approached by Marc, a very successful stockbroker, who read about some of the work I do and asked me to help him with peak performance—he did not mean his golf game but rather his business practice. I knew that I knew very little about the stock market, and I told him my work was pretty much circumscribed to helping athletes. However, he insisted that he was a high-performance broker and what he did was not that dissimilar from what my athletes were trying to do. I accepted his invitation to help him; I thought that if I could get him to articulate what his business practices were in the past and how they differ from the present, we might find some answers.

Marc then explained to me that, after receiving his MBA at Harvard, he went to New York City and got involved in the financial markets and made a lot of money over his fifteen-year career. With financial security, he decided to retire and move his family to San Diego. Once there, he found himself bored and, after the prompting of friends, decided to start a small brokerage firm. He brought on a junior partner, who he described as smart but not a genius. He admitted to micromanaging him by structuring a formula detailing exactly when to buy and sell stock and make certain exceptions. Everything was going well until the stock market crashed in 2002, when he lost 60 percent of his own assets as well as many millions of dollars invested by his clients.

Marc described getting very nervous about having failed his new clients and not having enough money to maintain his lifestyle. He felt tremendous pressure to make the money back, and the harder he tried, the more money he lost. His confidence began to spiral down and his personal life started to suffer. He described losing the assertiveness he once prided himself on and confessed that he was now unsure about any of his trades, always second-guessing himself. In time, he became so negative and desperate that he started implementing strategies he would find on the Internet and even consulted a psychic, all the while losing more and more of his own and his clients' money. Somehow he thought that I had some magic answer for him, but I did not. He asked me what I could do for him, and I told him that I would apply the same principles I use with athletes who had achieved great success in the past, but had inexplicably lost their ability to win.

I started to ask him probing questions, including how his junior partner was doing. Frustrated, Marc said that his partner was the only reason his firm was afloat.

Quizzically, I asked him, "Wasn't it you who taught your partner his skills?"

Rolling his eyes he said, "Exactly."

I then explained that I would like him to do four

homework assignments. In a moment of tension he looked at me as if I was trivializing his situation by asking him to do homework, and I assured him I was not. I explained that this seemingly simplistic process was what I utilized with Olympic champions. He accepted the challenge and we began.

His first assignment was to define the basic rules he had used before the market crashed, the rules he had used throughout his career. Marc came back the following week with a rather straight-ahead document that gave very clear parameters to trigger the buying and selling of stocks. He would buy blue-chip stocks when they reached a fifty-two-week low and simply sell them (that is, "stoploss") when they were down 5 percent from their next peak. He detailed that certain exceptional conditions allowed some deviation from the set parameters, but otherwise he generally never strayed from his template—he always stayed disciplined.

Then, I gave him his second assignment. I asked him to find out if his junior partner had modified the strict guidelines he taught him years ago. "I am sure he has—it was years ago, and we trade independently now." Nevertheless, I asked him to double-check.

The following week he came back and sheepishly said his junior partner was still using the exact same formula that he had been taught him. This response was confirmation about what I had already guessed: that he did not have a successful career on Wall Street for fifteen consecutive years by having good luck.

Defiantly he said, "That's right. It's about being smart, having good information, and being very disciplined when trading."

Then I facetiously asked him if he had had a brain stroke or if there were any reason to think he was neurologically or intellectually compromised.

"Of course not. I am in great shape mentally and physically."

I then asked him if there were any reason he should no longer be able to perform at the highest level.

"I guess not," he said.

I responded, "This is not about guessing; either there is a reason or there is no reason. Now which is it, and don't answer the question to me, answer to yourself."

In his third assignment, I asked him to trace his steps backward and see where he had gotten off track and deviated from the guidelines he had previously established. Not surprisingly, he figured out that it was right after the market crashed.

I then shared with him a story about a golfer who had been winning his club championship with only five holes left to play. On the 14th green the man had a simple ten-foot putt. He correctly read the break and made a good stroke, but the ball hit an old divot mark, kicked a little left, and missed the cup. The golfer immediately became anxious and rushed his stroke on the next putt, missed again and lost the hole. On the next green the golfer was nervous, pacing and repeating his practice stroke over and over. He had a short three-foot putt to tie the hole, but once again he rushed the stroke, pulled the putt, and missed left. On the next green he decided that he was not reading enough break on his putts and decided the ball would break eight inches rather than the four he saw. His putt missed again and soon he was on the last green, gripping and regripping his putter. If he missed the four-foot putt in front of him, he would miss his chance to secure the championship.

Visibly shaken, he amazingly changed his putting grip to cross-handed, a completely new grip, and hit the putt dead straight on line. The ball lingered on the lip of the cup and did not fall in.

He lost the club championship.

I asked the broker what he thought of the story, and Marc said, "Well, obviously the golfer got off track. All he needed to do was keep doing what he had been doing and not let the spike mark on the 14th green change his approach to putting."

"Exactly," I replied. I then told him that the number one reason people miss putts is not because of bad green reading or making bad strokes. It's a lack of commitment in executing the shot, which in turn creates inconsistency and undermines confidence. For example, there is a well-known occasion when Jack Nicklaus had to make a critical putt. He made a perfect putting stroke but the ball hit a bad patch of grass and veered off course. His playing partner later said, "Too bad you missed the putt." Jack replied, "I didn't."

His reply reinforced the notion that he made a good putt, his stroke was perfect, and he was fully committed to the shot. He did not undermine his own confidence by reacting to something that was out of his control (that is, a bad patch of grass).

I gave Marc his fourth and final homework assignment by asking him to focus on executing one task in his golf game the coming weekend: to make sure he was committed to every putt regardless of circumstance and difficulty. I emphasized that it did not matter if he was confused about how the greens' topography would cause the ball to break. All that mattered was that he stay completely committed to executing each shot. The following week, Marc and I got together. When he approached me he was smiling, even though the market had had another bad week. Why was he happy? Because he'd had the best putting round of his life and broke 80 for the first time.

Half-jokingly I asked him, "So is therapy over?"

He frowned with confusion.

I then explained that he now knew what he needed to

do with his stock trading business. "You want me to return and do what I did ten years ago and do what my junior partner does? It will take me years to make up my losses."

I pointed out that he could do whatever it is that he wanted, but maybe he was like the golfer in our story: He lost his patience and changed something that already worked. Unlike Jack Nicklaus, Marc undermined his own confidence when he hit a "bad patch" in the market by thinking he did something wrong. In golf terms, he never missed the putt; he only thought he did. He complicated a tried-and-true strategy that was successful for years after the market crashed. Often the greatest techniques, inventions, and interventions are surprising simple.

Over the next several months he reported making a little money, and by year's end he proudly said he had a good year. He gave me a nice bottle of red wine, thanking me for the counsel. The irony is that I only taught him to trust what he already knew—to trust his own mind and instincts, and not second-guess himself—and go back to the basics of what he knew.

KEEP IT SIMPLE, AGAIN?

The more complicated a task, the harder it becomes to trust yourself. Complexity creates doubt and makes us second-guess our own instincts. But if we keep it simple, trust comes naturally. Several years ago a young PGA Tour player visiting me was having some trouble with his short game and, in particular, putting. We were in the locker room and he was asking me about the best mental framework to maximize putting. As we were talking, golfing legend Billy Casper walked in. I said to the player, "Better than asking me, why don't we ask one of the greatest putters of all time?"

And Billy told this story: "In the 1965 Bob Hope Classic, I had a left edge, eight-foot putt to win the tournament. Directly behind the line of the putt sat President Eisenhower, someone I admired and wanted to meet."

The tour player impetuously interrupted the story and asked, "So, Mr. Casper, what did you do?"

Billy responded, "I hit the putt on the left edge, won the tournament, walked over, and shook the president's hand. The break is what it is, the speed is what it is, and I hit it on that line." Billy didn't ruminate or overanalyze things; he instinctively trusted his brain and body. He kept it simple.

In a subsequent conversation, Billy emphasized several things to me that make sense not only in golf, but in life: Keep things simple so you don't clutter your mind with extraneous nonsense. Trust your own innate ability; and most important, stay positive and believe in your own God-given ability.

One might argue that it is easy for Billy Casper to say those things, with fifty-one PGA Tour wins and three major championships under his belt. But it is these simple principles that provided Billy the framework for his enormous success in golf and in his life.

An easy but effective exercise to develop trust in your performance is to look at the task in its most simplistic form, see the task in your mind's eye, and simply transfer your visualization into action. This process of first visualizing and then physically re-creating what you've just seen in your mind's eye are basic principles put forth in Timothy Galloway's classic book *The Inner Game of Tennis*. When we overthink, we overanalyze, and this causes trepidation, which in turn undermines our performance. Our mind does best when it sees the whole of the situation—when we see the whole, we can simplify.

We have the ability to accomplish so much more in life when we learn to not let our minds get cluttered with complexity. If we know a way that works, then we must trust it. If we see something we can visualize doing, then we should go do it.

If you want to sell a product, see yourself engaging the customer and consummating the sale, and then without any hesitation, just go do it.

If you have a good approach to your business, don't change it because you had a rough situation that was out of your control.

Most sports and tasks in life do not require the acumen

of a brain surgeon; they only require trust in your own innate ability. Even a brain surgeon, in time, can figuratively and literally operate in his sleep; his well-trained mind simply knows how to perform brain surgery. In fact, during my residency, a very talented neurosurgeon friend of mine told me that he had evacuated so many subdural hematomas (blood on the brain) the night before that he wasn't sure if it was real or a dream. My friend's years of training had imprinted preferential neural circuits that guided his hands through the operations without always being consciously aware. If our brain can do this with the challenges inherent in neurosurgery, imagine what it can do for less complicated tasks.

Again, this is another example of the delicate balance between conscious and unconscious control. The surgeon, like the athlete, gets into trouble when he second-guesses himself and doubts what he already knows. Another example is if we think consciously about riding a bicycle, we will suddenly start to feel unsure in our pedaling. We ride a bicycle best when we don't think about how it is we pedal, but instead let ourselves enjoy the experience. When we practice enough, we can sit back and enjoy the beauty of the process that flows through us. That is the process of being able to trust our abilities, which lies at the essence of being in the Zone. Remember, "Those who think do not know, and those who know do not think."

We must trust our instincts, our creativity, and our vision. We must trust what we already know. If we do this, one day we may encounter a situation that requires us to do something simple but great, like hit a putt on the left edge, win the golf tournament, and shake the president's hand.

STAY IN THE NOW
AND BE IN
THE PROCESS

I never stressed winning . . .
I wanted the score to be a
by-product of practice.

—JOHN WOODEN

A t the Medina Golf Club on the Wednesday before the 2006 PGA Championship, Tiger Woods was on the practice green, putting under the watchful eyes of his coach Hank Haney. It was in the morning, and I was several feet away working with Rich Beem. Beemer, the 2002 PGA Champ, was being his ever-gregarious self and chatting it up with his friends and fans. There were thousands of people everywhere. Juxtaposed a few feet away was Tiger: practicing his putting.

During the next couple of hours, I noticed that Tiger did not once look up to talk to the media or other players; he never once broke his concentration. In fact, he did not say a word to Hank. He was completely involved in a simple putting drill. Over and over, he repeated the same stroke. And over and over, I heard the same mesmerizing sound of the ball rattling in the cup. Glassy eyed, he looked like he was in a trance. I even wondered if he was aware that anyone else was there.

I spent the rest of the afternoon with another player, and around 5:00 p.m., I was in the players' dining room eating with David Duval, Nick Price, and a sportswriter. I was talking to Nick about all the crazy attention that goes with defending a major golf championship and how difficult it must be to stay centered and focused. Nick emphasized that it was important to see the media for what it is and not get caught up in their opinions and the whole circus atmosphere. As I left the dining room, which was adjacent to the putting green, I was thinking about what a gentleman Nick Price is. I then looked up, and lo and behold, there was Tiger in the same place, doing the same drill, almost as if he had never left. He was so lost in the process; he made time look like it was standing still. After witnessing yet another display of his amazing focus and intensity, I was not surprised when he dominated the tournament and won it hands down.

Tiger's unique ability to utilize several Zone-enhancing

skills was also on display during the 2006 British Open. That week he won his eleventh major championship. During all the television interviews, he never talked about winning the tournament, but rather he talked about controlling the trajectory of his shots. His focus was on the process of what had led to his victory. Instead of getting caught up in the media frenzy and all the attention of his own historic success, he chose to stay focused on his goal of playing golf at the highest level. Tiger does not use the adoration of others to fuel his insatiable drive for excellence; his satisfaction comes from being a master of his own mind. He knows that the way to practice is to limit the focus of his mind on the task at hand. This allows him not to be separate from his experience but rather to become the experience. This is another example of what Zen masters call "direct experience."

Excelling in any sport or any other performance-related activity mandates that you must resist distractions of the mind—whether these distractions come before, during, or after your performance. These distractions might be internal, such as psychological fears, anxiety, or pangs of self-doubt. Or these distractions might be external, such as a chaotic environment surrounding you. When you are able to keep your mind still, staying precisely in the moment and not letting your attention waiver, you resist experiencing what the Zen masters refer to as "monkey mind," or noisy mind.

THE LESSON OF CHILDREN

Children provide us with a great example of how one resists monkey mind. When children play, they are completely engaged in the here and now. Their minds do not get stuck comparing themselves to their peers. They effortlessly transition their attention from one activity to the next, forgetting quickly what happened moments earlier and becoming completely absorbed in the present. They are able to make this transition seamlessly because their focus is on having fun and enjoying themselves. A boy hitting a baseball around the backyard is not distracted by a missed swing; rather he's focused on getting the ball again so he can hit the next home run. The young boy is not worried about the future or how he is perceived by others. He doesn't have time to; he is completely absorbed in the here and now. He is excited to be having fun in the moment, simply hitting baseballs.

Children teach us that the key to being in the moment (or being in the Zone) starts with having fun. When you are having fun, you often don't even hear your mother call you for dinner. You don't hear the bus whining down the street. You don't pay attention to the two or three other games being played on fields nearby. You simply play because you are enjoying yourself.

Children's ability to play and have fun comes naturally, without forethought or planning. Yet we all know that as we grow, mature, and our minds become more crowded and complicated, we tend to lose this innate connection to fun and play. And yet, we were all once children, so it stands to reason that we share this same innate gift.

CONSERVING ENERGY TO TIGHTEN YOUR FOCUS

We all require energy to keep our mind focused in the present and resist distraction. And yet, energy is a finite resource and must be conserved and then unleashed on demand if you are to perform your best. In golf, if you think of any other shot rather than the one you are about to execute, you are wasting a precious resource. All physical and mental activities expend energy. Emotions like anger and frustration drain us, as do thoughts that we can't control, such as worrying what will happen on the next shot. These debit our energy stores. Think of the emotionally wrenching experience of a mother worried that her child is lost or in danger. Even if she later learns that her child is safe and her worry was unnecessary, she still feels exhausted. In either case she has depleted her energy. We must use our energy wisely if we are to facilitate getting in the Zone. Worrying about the past or the future does not help the present situation. Overwhelming anxiety is an expensive experience. It drains us of the precious mental energy required to stay focused and transition our awareness from each moment to the next.

THE ONLY SHOT IN LIFE IS THE NEXT SHOT

In training golfers, I tell the pros there is only one shot you need to worry about, and that is the *next* shot. This attitude of staying focused on exactly what is in front of you—not behind you (in the past) or what is in the distant future—is of paramount importance in all performance-related activities. If a surgeon accidentally nicks an artery during a complicated surgery, he must immediately stop the bleeding and instantaneously transition his attention to the next emergent situation and sustain his focus. He does not have the time or luxury to lament his mistake, or his patient's life becomes in jeopardy. He must operate in the here and now to be successful.

In fact, it is when we move our awareness from the here and now into the future or the past that we create anxiety, which is one of the most consistent factors that keeps us from being engaged in the process, and being in the Zone. Imagine that your attention is focused on exactly what you are doing—preferably in this case reading this book. If you are absorbed in the process of reading, you are probably trying to figure out what in God's name is this wacky sports doctor talking about. Hopefully, you are interested, curious, and stimulated by what you read. However, if you are bored by this book and let your attention drift to the future, worrying about some life responsibility you haven't met, you start to generate anxiety.

And yet anxiety, as mentioned earlier, at times is inescapable; it's not a mystery. The trick is learning to manage our anxiety most effectively and keep it from becoming overwhelming.

Let's do a simple exercise so that you can see how easy it is to create anxiety:

Let your mind drift from reading, and focus about some future financial, medical, or legal concern. Take a moment and let this happen.

What do you feel?

Did you suddenly experience a pit in your stomach, a sense that anxiety is building?

Now, let your mind rest and drift back to thinking about the concepts in this book.

Start reading again, and soon your attention is back to the here and now, and your anxiety has dissipated.

This exercise demonstrates that it is the shift of attention away from the present that gives rise to anxiety. This is what we call an "anxiogenic" activity. A mother watching her son going off a ski jump is also an anxiogenic activity.

The beauty of this relationship between attention and anxiety is that it gives us a tool to manage anxiety. If you find yourself becoming anxious, all you have to do is let your attention drift back to the here and now and your anxiety will dissipate. When we manage our anxiety, we also conserve our energy. This simple redirection of attention sits at the core of most ancient meditative practices, whose goal is to conserve energy. These practices allow us to expend our energy on the next shot, rather than waste energy on some extraneous thought or emotion. It is the transitioning of attention from moment to moment that is critical in facilitating peak performance experiences.

THE TIGER TRANCE

Trance is the ability to be in two simultaneous realities at the same time. Like Tiger, we all have the ability to get into a trance. In the example of Tiger putting, he is completely absorbed in the putting drill, but he is also simultaneously aware of the other players practicing around him. He is in two realities, one where he is predominantly in his own world with his attention consciously focused on making a perfect putting stroke, and another where he is unconsciously aware of legions of fans yelling, "You the man." He hears everything but attends to nothing except the task at hand. This is a "Tiger trance."

We do this kind of split-reality thinking every day when we drive our car while talking on our cell phone: We are processing two worlds, driving and talking. Often we arrive at our destination perplexed, without the foggiest idea of how we got there. We wonder how our mind, while fully absorbed in conversation, was able to navigate each turn and react appropriately to each traffic signal without ever being consciously aware of the experience. It is truly amazing that our minds can process and act on the information, such as stopping at red lights and making various turns, while being completely absorbed in another task. This phenomenon is commonly called highway hypnosis. It is an example of everyday trance—something that almost all of us experience.

In this way, we all have the ability to process two worlds at once. We all have the ability to enter trancelike states, in which we block out internal or external distractions. The key to entering this mental state is to allow yourself to be *completely absorbed* in the task at hand. This is most easily accomplished when you are having fun with what you are doing. The ability to become completely entranced in a beautiful sunset or watching a thrilling movie is a gift. This gift of being absorbed in what you are doing is often ridiculed as daydreaming or being spacey. It is this gift of losing yourself in what you are doing that is essential for a Zone-like experience.

When a professional golfer is in the Zone, he may be aware of his position on the scoreboard and what hole he is playing, but if he wants to remain in the Zone he must keep his attention on the shot at hand. We have the innate ability to engage and create a dominant reality, like hitting the shot, and not engage in the nondominant reality, like monitoring the scoreboard and crowd reaction. A great example of this phenomenon comes from a famous story when Ben Hogan was playing with Claude Harmon on the 12th hole at the Masters in 1934. The hole is an infamous par 3, where winds swirl and crowds roar. Hogan hit his tee shot within twelve feet from the flagstick, and miraculously Harmon made the shot for a hole in one. As they walked up to the green, Hogan said nothing and methodically lined up his putt. Hogan made his putt for a birdie, and on the next tee said to Harmon, "That is only the second time I've birdied that hole."

The moral of the story is that Hogan was so deep in his own cocoon of concentration that he did not even notice or at least register that his playing partner had made an ace in the Masters in front of a large crowd. We all have the capacity to be aware of what is around us and simultaneously be fully engaged in another process—like the examples of highway hypnosis and Ben Hogan.

AVOID THE CULTURE OF ADD

We live in a culture of attention deficit disorder (ADD). We are bombarded with stimuli at all times, cell phones ringing, beepers going off, Game Boys and e-mail access at every destination. Our mind's attention is usurped by the seductive interface with modern-day technology. When our attention is pulled in every direction, we paradoxically live in an internal state of chronic inattentiveness. We may even find some bravado in seeing or showing off to others how many things we can do at once—as if multitasking is a sign of higher intelligence. This modern-day cultural phenomenon is toxic and leads to inefficiency and suboptimal performance. Driving a car to a destination that we know while on the cell phone is probably not a problem. The problem begins when we need to navigate to a new destination and concurrently engage in an important conversation. In this case, both tasks require our full attention. We are ill advised to utilize our split-mind trance ability and attend to one reality and not another. The end result is that both the quality of our conversation and our ability to drive suffer.

Generally, the quality of our performance is a function of the intensity of our focus. If you want to perform at the highest level, you must learn to become absorbed in the reality of what you are doing while unconsciously and simultaneously observing but not engaging in the reality of potential distractions around and within you.

CONTROLLABLE AND NONCONTROLLABLE
VARIABLES

In order to facilitate a peak performance experience, you have to use your common sense and resist distractions of all forms and not fall victim to cultural norms of multitasking behaviors. We must develop a healthy attitude toward life by engaging in some simple exercises that nurture process-oriented thinking.

Our attitudes toward competition are critical for our success. It is not a surprise that most people have an unhealthy attitude when it comes to "crunch time." Goals are the fulcrum that let us harness our energies and transform our efforts into achievements. It is human nature to see goals strictly in terms of results. However, in golf if you want to shoot the lowest score and win the tournament, you must understand that there are many components needed to make this goal realized. For example, to win a golf tournament you must shoot a great round. And on the PGA Tour that means a subpar score, a score that necessitates making more birdies than bogeys. However, to make a lot of birdies you must hit a lot of quality shots. In turn, quality shots require great concentration, blocking out all distractions and executing each shot with a clear image in mind. You must ask yourself: What is it that I want to do? Do I want to hit a draw or a cut? Is it 178 yards to the desired target on the back left shelf of the double-tiered green, or is it something else? You must be crystal-clear in your mind about what you are about to do. And it is equally important for you to be fully committed to executing each shot without distraction or ambivalence. It is this process that must happen over and over again for the player to reach his goal of shooting a great round of golf. If the golfer frames his goals in these terms, he is engaging in what is called *process-oriented* thinking. If the golfer only thinks of results or his score, he is engaging in *result-oriented* thinking. Result-oriented thinking brings many problems into play and is probably the most underrecognized and challenging problem I see in professional sports.

Process-oriented thinking is about doing the best you can; goal-oriented thinking is about beating someone or something. For example, if your goal in tennis is to beat your brother, then this result-oriented goal automatically narrows your chances for doing so. If the match is close, you will naturally start to think about the possibility of your pending victory. Your thoughts start to move to the future, and you start to feel that pit in your stomach. This emergence of additional anxiety causes your stroke to become tight and your balance awkward. Your chances for beating your brother lessen.

However, if your goal in playing your brother is to hit the smoothest shots and always maintain your balance, then beating him becomes an incidental consequence and not such a big deal. Your thoughts are much less likely to focus on the future, and you are less likely to choke. When you think strictly in terms of results, you open the possibility of doing everything perfectly and still losing. You may play impeccably and still lose to your competitor who scores better. However, if you focus on your effort or the quality of each shot, then you allow the possibility of winning even if your competitor beats you.

We cannot control what other players shoot; we cannot control an unpredictable gust of wind that flares up while our ball is airborne. There are many variables that we cannot control in sports, and in life. It is often said that the key to life is recognizing that only 10 percent of life is what happens to you, and 90 percent is how you react to it. When we judge ourselves by parameters that are influenced by events out of our control, we set ourselves up to damage our confidence, which by nature is very fragile and delicate. If we can learn to see experience as a combination of both controllable variables and noncontrollable variables, we maximize the opportunity to build confidence and not waste precious energy on negative thoughts and emotions.

A professional golfer cannot control a variety of things that influence whether he wins or loses a golf tournament. He cannot determine what his competitor does and what the weather is like. Imagine a player hitting a perfect shot, only to find that it has burrowed into a divot in the middle of the fairway. The typical emotional response is to get upset about the bad break, which in turn only hurts any chance of hitting the next shot well. Great competitors learn to identify what variables are integral to their performance and which ones are within their power to influence. It is the discipline of differentiating controllable and non-controllable variables that allows you to expand your energy most efficiently and productively. A simple exercise I ask Tour players to engage in is what I call the *two scorecards*.

TWO SCORECARDS

Several years ago I developed a practical exercise for players on the PGA Tour. It is designed to help them shift their perspective from result goals to process goals. I ask the golfer to begin the day by using two scorecards: the traditional scorecard that records the player's actual score (his results), and a second scorecard, to record the percentage of shots that he executed to the best of his ability. Golf, like many tasks in life, allows you the time to choose when you take action. In golf when it is your turn to execute (hit your shot), you have the choice to back away if you are not fully committed, then refocus and start over. You have the opportunity to step out of the shot if you experience negative thoughts during your swing. Theoretically, this allows the player to hit every shot with full commitment and clarity.

I often ask golfers to record the process component by

scoring a simple yes or no to the following questions. These questions are applied to each shot:

1. First, did you visualize the shot you wanted to hit before executing it?
2. Second, did you hit the shot without any doubt or ambivalence (fully committed)?
3. Last, did you back away from the shot and let your mind clear if you incurred any negative or distracting thoughts?

If the golfer can answer yes to every one of his shots that day, he scores 100 percent on his process scorecard. If he answers no to any of the above, that shot is recorded as a no. It is the ratio of yes to no that determines the quality of his process and in turn determines the quality of his performance and ultimate score.

Often, even at the highest level, PGA Tour professionals will report to me that on only 60 percent of the shots that day were they able to accomplish a yes, which means they either had not had a clear image or were not fully committed to 40 percent of their shots.

I then ask them another very simple question: "You have just told me that of the 70 shots you hit today, only 42 (60 percent) were executed with full commitment and a clear mind. Do you think we could bump that up to 75 percent of your shots?"

Uniformly the players always say yes, because this goal of staying process-oriented is within the control of the athlete. For the most part, the professional golfer has the ability to choose to execute the shot when his mind is crystal clear, without any doubt lurking in his unconscious. The main variables that determine his result are within his sphere of influence and mastery. His mental energy is used most efficiently and productively when he invests it in process goals and not result goals. However, the paradox is that if you always evaluate yourself in terms of identifying if you are in the process or not, you prevent yourself from being absorbed in the task. We live in the process when we stop evaluating our performances and just have fun doing the task.

When an athlete invests his energy in this way, he is more likely to develop a sense of mastery and build confidence. He can take solace in knowing that even if he did not win the tournament, he hit a very high percentage of shots the way he wanted to and thus experiences a sense of satisfaction that is rewarding and reinforcing. In contrast, if he is strictly result-oriented, he can theoretically hit every shot to the best of his ability, score great, and still lose, thus causing his psyche to experience failure rather than reward. This human predilection to be strictly result-oriented is toxic to the elite performer. When you stay more process-oriented and focus on mastering the controllable variables, you inevitably accomplish greater results.

You can use this type of exercise to evaluate the efficiency of your effort. The more efficient your effort, the better your performance and the more you build confidence.

FOCUSING ON THE CONTROLLABLE

The importance of differentiating controllable and noncontrollable variables is enormous. Let's take a very common life situation like divorced parents fighting over the custody of their child. Almost uniformly both parents will voice that their focus and goal is to provide the best life for their child. Inevitably, some event occurs where one parent becomes enraged with the other parent. Maybe the one parent loses their job and cannot pay for support for several months, causing the other to engage legal action resulting in a ruling that changes the custody arrangement. The court ruling may cause one parent to become so angry that they unconsciously change their behavior toward their child and become obsessed with getting back at their ex-spouse. Their precious energy is no longer directed toward loving their child, but rather is sucked into a bottomless abyss of anger and resentment. This kind of cycle can self-perpetuate and become stronger and exponentially toxic.

Let's continue and say that in this example, the parent who lost their job is unwilling to accept that the judge's recent ruling is outside of their control. The energy of their anger does nothing to help their predicament. In fact, the more they allow their attention to focus on something they see as not fair, in this case a variable they cannot control, the more they lose mastery of the situation. Their energy would be better spent on making sure they find a good job and restoring their previous ability to pay child support on time. It is this action that will lead to their desired result. We must focus on the things we can change and not become consumed with the things we cannot.

To develop this ability, you start by choosing a goal and define what variables are within your control and what variables are not within your control. For example, imagine going to a job interview. You can control how well you prepare and how appropriately you dress and behave, but you cannot control whether the interviewer likes you or if you get the job. If you prepare and answer the interviewer's questions to the best of your ability and solely judge yourself on this aspect, you create a self-reinforcing cycle of building confidence and competence regardless of the interview's outcome.

Learn to get in the process by following these three simple rules:

1. *Always try to have fun!* Let yourself become absorbed in the task at hand. We fall into self-induced trance states that allow us to block out distractions when we are having fun.

2. *Conserve your energy.* Learn to differentiate what variables involved in your performance (or task) you have control over, and focus on them, not the other ones.

3. *Live in the process.* Institute the "two scorecard" exercise in all performance-related activities and judge yourself on your effort, and you will never feel like you have lost control. You will think like a winner, and your confidence will build.

If you take the time once a month to apply these rules to one goal, you will slowly but surely begin to learn how to judge yourself on the most important variables—the ones you control. You will learn that your results are better by paying less attention to them and more attention to the process of what you are doing. If you find that you cannot stay in the process and are fixated with a poor past result, you must learn that your fixation stems from your inability to accept the reality of this result. Paradoxically, when we learn to accept a difficult reality, we free ourselves to move on and create something new. Keep learning to stay process-oriented in school, in business, and in sports. You will find that this new perspective allows you to become fully absorbed in each task. You may even find that you feel time is standing still. With great focus and a clear understanding of where your efforts should be directed, you become trance-like, and the monkey in your mind will be no more.

LESSON SIX

MANAGE YOUR EMOTIONS AND THOUGHTS

If you find yourself in a hole, stop digging.

—OLD ZEN SAYING

Over the past twenty years of practicing psychiatry, I have always been fascinated by how human beings relate to themselves. Think of the caricature of the emotional Italian man who defines himself by what he feels. In contrast, think of the cerebral professor who defines himself by what he thinks. Are we what we think or are we what we feel?

The answer is neither. We are always *more* than what we think and what we feel. And yet often we don't experience ourselves that way; indeed, powerful thoughts and intense emotions can make us believe that we are that thought or that feeling. When our body is sick, let's say we have strep throat, we do not assume that our throat will be sore forever. We know it is a symptom that alerts us to see the doctor. We think of the pain in our throat as being separate from who we are as a person. When it comes to our bodies, we know we are more than what we feel. However, when it comes to our minds, we lose the capacity to see ourselves objectively.

In order to manage our emotions and thoughts under pressure, we must master intense feelings and not let them master us. This is crucial for being able to drop into the Zone during competition. The first thing you must do to be a great champion is separate your awareness from your thoughts and feelings. For example, look directly in front of you and you may see this book or a picture on the wall. The images before you fill—and define—your awareness in this moment. However, when you close your eyes and the images disappear, your awareness continues. In this way, you need not be defined by the emotions or thoughts you experience. Paying attention to your own awareness gives you this power.

THE NEUROTIC CONTINUUM

The mind is distinctly different from the body because we experience the world through our minds, and it is inherently difficult to keep the lens that we look through free from distortion. So though our mind is similar to our body in the sense that it too can experience symptoms, such as frustration or worrying more frequently, it is harder to gain that objective distance from what we are feeling. Am I worried for no reason at all? Am I able to handle all this pressure? What is wrong with me? These thoughts may indicate that a person is under increased stress, but often he is so attached to the thought and accompanied feeling, he feels as if he *is* the feeling.

When you go to see a therapist and tell him or her your problems, hoping for some answers and a way to alleviate your pain, the good therapist listens quietly, asks insightful questions, and then sits back in order to reflect and allow you to understand yourself. Astute therapists will guide you to experience your worries from a different perspective. They will help you separate the forest from the trees. Therapists help people not by giving their opinions, but rather by asking certain questions that nudge clients into seeing their thoughts, emotions, and life in a different way, a way that is more objective.

This process, of helping the individual see the forest from the trees, is technically called helping the client develop an observing ego. It takes knowledge to realize that you have a choice to simply be aware and not react to your emotions or thoughts. I like to call this ability "know-mind" awareness. The idea being that our greatest wisdom is not from our thought, but rather from developing a greater awareness of ourselves. Often we find that our minds are inundated with negative, racing thoughts that arise from unrealistic fears. These thoughts are self-perpetuating and create more fear, which fuels more negative and distorted thoughts. If we are able to take a moment and step back and look at the bigger picture, we may see that we are being neurotic; yet we still have a difficult time believing what we see.

It is our know-mind awareness that allows us to observe our thoughts and see if they make sense or not, enabling us to differentiate ourselves from our thoughts just as we differentiate ourselves from our physical symptoms—such as that of a sore throat. For instance, if our throat is sore and sick, we don't automatically jump to the conclusion that we, as a whole, are sore and sick. And yet, we often don't make this distinction when it comes to our so-called emotional symptoms. If we feel bad, confused, or lacking in confidence, sometimes we jump to the conclusion that we are bad, confused, or unable to succeed. When we learn to differentiate ourselves from our emotions, we can learn to become the master of both our feelings and our thoughts, paving the path to self-actualization.

For example, in therapy you learn to become aware of reoccurring patterns—of behaviors, thoughts, and feelings. You may be negativistic or overly optimistic, but rarely do you see reality without distorting it with your own biases. I always say that objective reality is something only God is

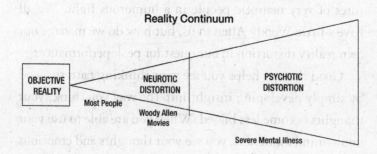

privy to, and the rest of us distort our reality as a function of our past experiences, genetics, and perceptual abilities; indeed, we all distort reality to varying degrees, defining where we sit on the reality continuum. See the picture above.

Psychosis is when reality is tremendously distorted. The psychotic person (or person suffering from some sort of temporary psychosis) hears voices, or becomes paranoid—they imagine things that are not there. Neurosis is when reality is less distorted, and all of us are to some degree neurotic. For example, when we meet a new person who reminds us of someone in our past, we color the experience with our own bias. We distort reality. If we liked the person in our past, we may bias the immediate encounter in a positive light. If we did not like the person, we are likely to bias our perception negatively. This all occurs without our conscious awareness. This example of a mild distortion is universal, and it is the degree of distortion that correlates with the degree of our neurosis. Every experience we have is influenced by our own bias. Woody Allen movies present caricatures of very neurotic people in a humorous light. We all have a little Woody Allen in us, but how do we manage our own reality distortion in our quest for peak performance?

Good therapy helps you see your thinking patterns, and by simply developing insight into the way you think, your thoughts become less biased. When you are able to use your know-mind awareness, you see your thoughts and emotions like when you sit in the cinema watching the previews, waiting for the movie to start. When you learn to engage an essential tool to experience your thoughts and feelings as part of you, but not as the only thing that defines you; this is crucial for managing performance of any kind, whether that be in life, business, or sport.

The ability to see with your know-mind awareness can be developed through many avenues including physical training, meditation (mental training), and spiritual practices. When you develop this ability, thoughts and emotions become waves that dissipate on the shores of your consciousness. This is the essence of know-mind awareness and it is a fundamental prerequisite to being in the Zone.

CATASTROPHIZING: THE LINK BETWEEN
THOUGHT AND EMOTION

Our thoughts are often fueled—if not created—by our emotions. We must understand that thoughts and emotions are inextricably interwoven. If we think positively, we start to feel better; conversely, but just as true, if we feel bad, we start to think negatively. This simple reciprocal relationship between thought and emotion sits at the foundation of what is called cognitive therapy. When people go to psychiatrists and psychologists and share depressing and negative thoughts, the clinician will ask the client to do a reality check and evaluate the accuracy of their own thoughts. For example, let's imagine a boy strikes out three times in a little league game and feels bad. He starts berating himself by thinking he cannot hit, that he is a bad baseball player, or even a bad athlete. In this example he lets his poor performance on one given day generalize, and he starts to catastrophize.

I encourage all clients, not only athletes, to mobilize their know-mind awareness (their observing ego) and do a reality check. In this hypothetical case we would ask the boy if he struck out because he is a bad player, or because he might have had a bad day? Are you really bad at all sports? And why do you think that?

Often he might say that striking out three times is terrible, especially because the last three games he has hit well. The boy starts to give us data that shows where his catastrophizing begins. We ask him to review what he's saying, and based on reality, reframe his initial statement and thoughts. After he reframes the experience, we ask him how he feels and invariably he says he feels better. This ability to reframe is know-mind awareness in action.

Dave Binn is an All-Pro long snapper for the San Diego Chargers NFL football team. The job of a long snapper is among the most stressful positions in football. The long snapper, like a field goal kicker, is on the field for only a few plays per game. However, often it is those few plays that are most critical and determine the game's fate. When Dave Binn snaps for a game-winning field goal with millions watching, there is no margin for error and no room for self-doubt. A bad snap at the wrong time and your NFL career could be over. Recently, after a friendly game of golf and an ensuing discussion about the mental aspects of sports, I asked my friend Dave if he had ever had bad thoughts in playoffs or other championship games. Being the mellow but straight-ahead guy he is, he promptly said of course, but immediately followed by saying he never snaps the ball with a negative thought. He explained that if he needs to, he simply brings forth memories of all the great snaps he has made over his career, and these memories put him in the right frame of mind.

It is no accident that big Dave Binn is an NFL All-Pro. He shows us a perfect example of using his know-mind awareness by recognizing counterproductive thoughts and reframing them with the help of past positive experiences. Binn's reflexive ability to do this in competition is what I call impeccable mental hygiene.

JIMMY SHEA: A FALLING LEAF

So the question remains, how do we develop the ability to use our thoughts and emotions to help us and avoid letting them get in the way of reaching our potential? A wonderful example of handling difficult emotions comes from my clinical work at the U.S. Olympic Training Center in San Diego, California, with Jimmy Shea. I am fortunate that Jimmy has given me his permission to discuss our work together. In 2001, Dr. James Bauman, a good friend and chief sports psychologist at the training center, referred Jimmy to me for evaluation and treatment. Jimmy was a past world champion in the winter sport called Skeleton, in which a single person goes headfirst on a sled down an icy track at speeds over 80 miles per hour.

When I first met Jimmy, he was in the media spotlight and under a great deal of pressure. He was America's first third-generation Olympian: His dad, Jim Sr., was an Olympian, as was his grandfather Jack, who won two gold medals in speed skating in 1932. Jimmy was voted by the U.S. Olympic athletes to read the Olympic Oath at the opening ceremonies in Park City, Utah, and carry the torch. However, only seventeen days before the games, his grandfather was killed in a tragic automobile accident. Jimmy was very close to his grandfather and was immobilized by sadness and anger. With only days left before the Olympics, it became clear that Jimmy needed to find a way to channel and sublimate these overwhelming feelings if he wanted to perform well in the most important race of his life.

Clearly, this was not an easy task for anyone, let alone for someone who was now in the center of the public eye. Initially, Jimmy experienced the normal stages of bereavement: disbelief, depression, and anger. Understandably this tragedy undermined his focus and motivation for the Olympics. The impact looked like it would have a paralytic effect on Jimmy's performance. Although normally effective for mildly traumatic experiences, Jimmy's natural instinct to suppress difficult emotions was not enough because of the magnitude of his feelings.

Jimmy needed more in the next seventeen days—he needed to work through these difficult feelings and channel the emotional energy in a positive direction. Everyone, including Jimmy, who experiences anger does so because he or she has been hurt. We feel hurt when we are violated and lose trust in something we love. Jimmy started to understand that nature of his pain. He learned that its magnitude was in proportion to the love for his grandfather and that although his grandfather was not physically present, Jimmy still deeply felt his spirit.

This critical insight catalyzed a flood of beautiful memories of his grandfather helping him, which in turn recharged and reinvigorated his compromised motivation. Jimmy placed the funeral picture of his grandfather inside his helmet prior to the race. When the final race came, he was among the last to compete and needed an awesome time to win, which seemed increasingly unlikely because snow, which slows the track significantly, had started to fall. However, Jimmy was completely absorbed and inspired to have the opportunity to honor his grandfather's spirit. With his grandpa's picture in his helmet, Jimmy fired out of the starting gate with a controlled fury and forged one of sport's most indelible images, winning the gold medal by a 500th of a second, taking off his helmet, and showing the world the photograph of his grandfather and his victory smile. Jimmy Shea found the Zone that day by sublimating the energy of his raw emotion into his performance.

In Jimmy's case, he had only two and a half weeks to work through his feelings. However, when emotion erupts in the heat of battle, you often do not have the luxury of time. You have to manage your emotion in the heat of the moment. A concept I like to share when helping golfers faced with this challenge is to ask them to metaphorically think about anger as if it were like holding a hot coal. If you hold it too long you will get burned, so you must drop it. It is okay to get upset at the last shot and embrace the feeling for a moment, but it is not okay to take that anger to the next shot. It takes mental discipline to learn to slow down and let the feeling pass.

I even sometimes ask players to shut their eyes and

imagine putting their anger on a falling leaf and releasing it to descend into a flowing stream. I ask them to visualize the leaf carrying the emotion away, downstream, and then to open their eyes and get ready for the next shot.

REPLACE FRUSTRATION WITH CURIOSITY

Aside from the intensity of pain or anger, another emotion that can often get in the way of being able to access or stay in the Zone is frustration, and thankfully there is a fairly simple, straightforward tool to use in situations when your frustration seems to be taking over your focus and ability to perform: This process is called *thought substitution*. I observed this phenomenon at the 2007 U.S. Open Golf Championships in Oakmont, Pennsylvania. I was walking inside the ropes during a Wednesday practice round with Rich Beem and Steve Elkington. Steve, who is a past PGA champion, seemed to be getting every bad break imaginable. However, instead of getting frustrated, he expressed a look of curiosity. At one hole in particular, he hit a perfect drive only to find that his ball had rolled two inches too far into unplayable rough—another horrible break.

Beem's caddie, Billy Heim, and I simultaneously observed how Steve dealt with the situation. He did not moan or groan or get angry, but his face revealed a sense of curiosity. Creatively, he hooded his club, and while Billy and I looked on in bewilderment, he hit a great shot, demonstrating how his curiosity resulted in success.

When you stay frustrated, you do not think as well. Conversely, when you try to substitute curiosity, you tend to think creatively and conquer the task at hand.

DEVELOPING YOUR KNOW-MIND AWARENESS

So far we have reviewed two visualization tools as well as one conceptual tool: imagining your anger embodied in the image of holding a hot coal and picturing your emotion or thought floating downstream on a leaf. A third visual technique is to employ what is called an attentional shift.

Prior to my match for the 1976 National Junior Table Tennis Championship, tennis great Pancho Gonzales told me to pick a spot far out on the horizon—whether it be in a gym, a stadium, a conference room, or on a golf course. He said to concentrate on that point until my mind became still. He continued by suggesting if and when my attention shifted back to some stressful emotion or thought to simply refocus it on the point again, and the thought or emotion would pass. This simple exercise quickly made my mind, as it will yours, transition away from stress-induced emotions and thoughts and find relaxation even in the most intense situations. This exercise expands our awareness and, like many meditative techniques, involves distancing one's awareness from one's own thoughts and emotions. If your mind is absolutely still, you can experience your awareness as the gap between two thoughts, then you are in the Zone.

Sometimes breathing techniques are helpful in finding that still moment. When we breathe fast and tight, like a panting dog, we move dead air and do not oxygenate our lungs, creating a vicious cycle that reinforces feeling anxious and racing thoughts. If we turn our attention to our breath and breathe rhythmically, we can imagine ourselves looking like and feeling like the Pillsbury Doughboy. Now imagine yourself with a soft belly, as your diaphragm engages, pulling air deep into your lungs, relaxing you and stilling your mind. This is in essence a yogic breath. I ask athletes to put their hand on their belly and make sure it feels soft, without tension. If it is not, I ask them to engage in yogic breathing.

Checking in with our whole body, not only our breath, is very important. Sometimes when we perform poorly, we slump into a poor posture, which in turn perpetuates the depressed feeling and we lose focus and lament. If we walk with our heads up and with good posture regardless of our performance, we tend to feel better and increase the probability of a better performance on our next attempt. There exists a natural bidirectional relationship between our body and our mind. They both influence each other without our conscious awareness being involved. This relationship is something we can take advantage of to perform better. For example, our hands often tell us about our own internal state.

If the athlete is stretching his fingers, it signifies that he is about to create and achieve. In contrast, if his hands are fumbling and clammy, he feels nervous and apprehensive. The simple act of stretching out your fingers relieves tension.

THRIVING DURING COMPETITION

It is important to realize that whatever emotion you experience in the heat of battle, you are best off moderating it and trying not to get too excited. As Yoga Berra said, "It isn't over until it's over." If you find yourself thinking about winning before it occurs, remember another Zen saying, "Victory is for the one who has no thought of himself."

The Zen Master Shunryu Suzuki talks about the need to not care for excessive joy. He states that when you can do this, you will have "imperturable composure." In lay terms, this means if you find yourself on the verge of doing something great that could transform your life, you must not allow yourself to bask in these seductive thoughts or you will lose your composure.

Managing your thoughts requires constant attention. For example, if you are challenged by a sport like golf, with long periods of downtime between each shot, you must learn to pulse your concentration so you do not burn out. I often advise golfers to think of an accordion as a visual metaphor, relaxing after each shot and then contracting as they build their concentration, approaching the next. The most efficient way to study is not to study continuously for consecutive hours at a time, but rather to take fifteen-minute breaks each hour to refresh your mind. The idea is to maximize the quality of the activity, not the quantity, and to do this you must always try to keep your mind relaxed and ready.

In essence, the most effective way to manage difficult emotions and thoughts in competition or in life is to develop the ability to slow down when agitated and become conscious of your reaction. This process of seeing your emotions and thoughts separate from yourself is the basis of your know-mind awareness.

KNOW-MIND RULES AND TOOLS FOR DEALING WITH DIFFICULT EMOTIONS AND THOUGHTS

WHEN IN THE HEAT OF BATTLE:

1. Slow down your pace.
2. Visualize placing the disturbing thought or emotion on a leaf and let it float downstream.
3. Utilize an attentional shift technique (like Pancho Gonzales).
4. Do a body check—correct your posture, stretch your fingers, and breathe with a soft belly.
5. If angry, imagine holding a hot coal and dropping it.

6. If frustrated, substitute curiosity (like Steve Elkington).
7. Learn to pulse your concentration to avoid burnout.
8. Don't think ahead (be like Yogi Berra, "It isn't over until it's over").
9. Remember positive past experiences (like Dave Binn).

WHEN YOU HAVE TIME TO REFLECT:

10. Embrace the difficult emotion and transform its energy (like Jimmy Shea).
11. Utilize the ability to cognitively reframe (like the little league boy who strikes out).

If, for example, you are in the heat of the moment and need to deal with some difficult emotion or thought, you can reference rules 1 through 9. For example, you can use thought substitution by substituting the feeling of anger with curiosity. Or you can use one of the visualization techniques by imagining your anger as a hot coal in hand which needs letting go.

Similarly, if you need to let go of either bad thoughts or feelings, you can engage in yogic breathing or attentional shift techniques, like concentrating on a distant object.

If you have some time to process difficult emotions

before the big performance, you can sublimate the emotion by embracing it and tracing it to its origin, thus transforming the energy of a negative emotion into a synergistic force, like Jimmy Shea (see rule 10). If bad thoughts are the challenge, you can take the time to list all the relevant data, look for any cognitive distortions in your thinking, and do a cognitive reframe like our little league baseball player (rule 11).

All of these tools listed are techniques that you can master with a little effort. You can practice these tools the next time you need to perform and are bothered by distractions. You will learn that when you practice these tools, you are mobilizing and developing your know-mind awareness and thus training your mind to become more Zone-like. The Zone-enhancing tool of being able to access your know-mind awareness is not only invaluable in sports, but in all of life.

KEEP YOUR MOTIVATION PURE

There are two levers for moving
men—interest and fear.

—NAPOLEON BONAPARTE

love it when I am at a baseball game and people shout "Keep bringing it" as the pitcher throws a 100-mile-per-hour fastball. Similarly, when a great guitarist like Santana is letting loose a fiery guitar riff, he too is "bringing it." Both performers are letting their juice flow through them, becoming mere conduits to their own passionate energy. They simply surrender to their gift. When they allow this kind of flow state, they are not separate from the experience, much like our example of Tiger Woods putting in a trance. This is the

Zone. It is a place where the pressure of others, including our own, does not exist. When we surrender to the experience and let it happen, we usually end up victorious. The Zone is about the here and now and not some other place or concern. A mind that is worried about what others think or is constantly evaluating his or her performance and comparing it to that of others puts up a blockade to the Zone. This comparative thought process, of judging one's self in relation to others, cuts us off from the "juice," and the Zone evaporates. I like to say to my players, "The higher the bar, the purer the motivation." And indeed, this link between performance and motivation is an essential ingredient to finding the "plug-in" for your own juice and staying in the Zone.

INTRINSIC VERSUS EXTRINSIC MOTIVATION

When our motivation comes from anywhere other than our heart and dreams, it still serves us, but its power is limited. We will not have access to the insatiable drive that comes from the infinite energy of *intrinsic motivation*. Conversely, *extrinsic motivation* is when our drive comes from the external reality where things like the media, criticism, or material gain and fame matter most. Extrinsic motivation limits your energy for getting into the Zone of life.

On the other hand, if your motivation comes from the world of the heart and soul—your deepest connection to yourself—you begin to nurture and access an almost limit-less supply of motivation and Zone energy.

Let's take one high-profile example from the world of business and technology. Bill Gates, a man whose fame and fortune are unparalleled, was first a computer nerd with a dream. Fascinated with computers, he was determined to find a way to apply his passion for computers to the real world. In 1968 he started mischievously playing with and hacking into the school's computer, which in turn caused the computer to frequently crash. When the cause of the crashes became known, Bill was ironically offered unlim-ited computer time in return for providing help to main-tain the computer's function. Bill Gates is quoted as saying, "It was when we got free time at C-cube (Computer Center Corporation) that we really got into computers. I mean, and then I became hard-core. It was day and night."

By 1973 he was enrolled at Harvard University, yet within one year he dropped out and walked away. It must have taken tremendous courage and deep belief in himself in order to have made such an astonishing decision. To bor-row from the great poet Robert Frost, Bill Gates had truly taken "the road less traveled." Why?

He saw his dream and he went for it. He didn't listen to the naysayers, the doubters, the criticizers. He listened only to himself, followed his passion, and kept his motivation pure. The decision to leave Harvard enabled Bill Gates to go out on his own and start a small company on a shoestring budget, a company called Microsoft that grew and grew and grew. And as we all know, Microsoft changed the world as we know it.

Bill Gates was not motivated extrinsically, but intrinsically. He did what his heart told him to do even at the expense of risking a Harvard education. But his courage created a pure motivation that allowed him to reach the highest level and serves him to this very day.

And yet listening to that voice, believing in it, and sticking with it is not always easy.

ALL THE TALENT IN THE WORLD

Two years ago I was contacted by a very successful forty-nine-year-old businessman who wanted me to help him with his golf game. Let's call him Paul. Right away, I explained to Paul that I normally work either with young developing players or Tour professionals. He responded emphatically that money was no object, and he assured me he was a great player, citing some pretty impressive statistics, including a subpar scoring average and winning two state amateur titles. I gave in and told him to meet me at my golf club the next week.

The following Friday, we met at the golf club. As we passed through the locker room on our way to the course, Paul's eyes almost popped out of his head when he caught sight of Phil Mickelson's locker. On the way to the course he asked me about other famous athletes who belong to the club. Although my club does have a fairly impressive membership roster, I found it curious that he seemed more focused on the membership than on his golf game.

On the first tee he striped his tee shot about 300 yards down the middle and five hours later he casually carded a six-under-par 66. He was the real deal. He had all the talent in the world. He was a big strong guy, a great athlete, good touch, charismatic, and wealthy to boot. I was a bit confused why a guy this good, who had won two state amateur titles in his youth, had not made his way to the Tour.

He explained that when he was younger, he had been to qualifying school seven times and had never made it through the second stage. Then he shamefully admitted that he had always choked and fallen apart when he had been on the precipice of getting to the next level. He told me that for the last ten years he had been focused on making money, and with a sly smile he said he had made a lot, but now he was determined to dedicate himself to getting a Senior PGA Tour card.

Although he told me only a few, seemingly casual details explaining why he had not made it on Tour, I was beginning to put two and two together.

After the round, we had a drink together and he casually said, "Doc, I don't understand it. I have beaten all these guys in practice, big-money games, and amateur tournaments, and I know that I am a better athlete and a better golfer, yet I have never been able to reach my potential."

I responded by empathizing how frustrating that must be.

He responded passionately, "You're right—all I have ever wanted to do was to become a famous golfer."

I stopped him and said, "Famous golfer, or the best you can possibly be?" My question made him look like a deer in the headlights. He looked kind of embarrassed. His words had actually revealed his true unconscious motivation: Paul did not want to be the *best* golfer he could be; he wanted to be a *famous* golfer.

If fame is your primary goal, you undermine the motivation required to become truly great. If you want to compete at the level of the PGA Tour, you need to have pure motivation. Greatness takes unbridled passion for the task at hand, which means pure motivation. If you play for passion, you play for fun. You don't care what others think, you play because you want to, like kids playing baseball in the backyard. That is the essence of pure motivation.

In contrast, when you play a sport because you desire to become famous, you actually undermine your own ability to realize your potential. Why is this so? Because when we seek fame and adoration, we are trying to fill a need. This basic need for approval from other people is part of the human condition. When we seek approval, whether it be conscious or unconscious, we set ourselves up to be at the beck and call of too many masters. Fierce competition has such intense demands that adding more pressure only leads to overload and failure. Caring what others think separates us from the direct experience at hand. When we do this, we cannot mobilize know-mind awareness and we cannot be in the Zone.

I asked Paul if he had seen the movie *Last Samurai*. Fortunately he had and we talked about the scene in which Tom Cruise is in the midst of a losing sword battle with his teacher, a master samurai, who tells him that he has "too many minds." Cruise's character was "minding" the people watching and what they were thinking; he was also minding the enemy, and he was minding his sword.

"You must have no mind," says the teacher.

Paul has at least "two" many minds. He wants to be famous first and foremost; being the best golfer came second. I explained to him that greatness and fame are two different things, with two different paths. The path to becoming famous only occasionally leads to the path of greatness. It is healthiest when fame comes as a by-product from pursuing your goal, but it should not be the goal in and of itself. I added that if fame was truly what he wanted, he would be better off seeing a public relations firm instead of a peak-performance doctor.

Oddly, when Paul left, I could see that he was not upset,

but almost relieved. I had the distinct impression that he had found what he was looking for: an explanation of why, with all the talent in the world, he had not become a PGA Tour player.

PLAYING FOR SOMEONE ELSE

There are many ways in which we can muddy the waters of our motivation, clouding our vision and undermining our ability to reach our goals. In Paul's case, he focused on achieving fame rather than simply being the best golfer he could be; this simple displacement of his energy on an external goal, fame, undermining his ability to realize his potential.

Another way we interrupt the purity of our motivation is when we play in order to please someone else—a parent, a coach, a partner. This situation is typified by a young professional golfer on the LPGA whom I help. She is very humble and sweet. She loves playing golf and became a professional for all the right reasons—her passion for the game, her love of competitive sports, and the pleasure she gets from playing golf.

But at our first meeting she immediately articulated what her difficulties were. She told me she loved golf, but she worried a lot about what her parents thought. She told me that her mother frustrates her with questions like, "Why did you hit the ball in the water on that shot?" And she would futilely try to explain to her mom that it was not her intention to hit a bad shot.

The "net-net" of our very first conversation was to help her see that she probably would not be able to change her mom's reaction to her golf shots. But she could help herself by changing her reaction to her mom. Most important, she must learn that the negative comments of her mother are only words, and in and of themselves they are powerless unless she (the player) gives them meaning and takes them to heart.

Many of us have negative thought patterns that play like tape loops in our minds, but we have the choice to evaluate these thoughts and dismiss them or integrate them into our psyche and pay the price. My LPGA player can learn to devalue the unhealthy comments her mom makes and value the supportive ones. She can do this because she instinctively knows that thoughts of caring so much about what others think are counterproductive to her pursuit of becoming a great athlete.

You can choose who and what you listen to if you pay attention to your instincts. Resist pandering to the reactions of others. Have the courage to keep your motivation pure and the strength and discipline to resist caring about what others think about you.

BECOMING AN ARCHITECT OF YOUR OWN REALITY

When we care too much about what others think, we essentially displace our pure motivation. Instead, we learn to rely on *fear* as our primary motivator. Although we can benefit from fear-based motivation, it is not the type of motivation that sets the stage for getting in the Zone. We call this type of motivation external or extrinsic. In contrast, when our motivation comes organically from within, it is called intrinsic, and this is the "pure motivation" we all seek.

So what is the right mind-set to get in the Zone? Is it best to be confident and cocky or timid and humble? Are the great performers completely engulfed in their own world and if so, is that behavior bad or narcissistic?

Let's start by addressing the question of arrogance and the concept of narcissism. The word narcissistic is derived from the Greek myth about a handsome young man, Narcissus, who is unknowingly punished by the gods when he becomes obsessed with his image reflecting in a pond. He is tortured by this fate because he can no longer distinguish his reflection from himself. His reality becomes an illusion. The word narcissism has a derogatory meaning, but the literal meaning is the character trait of self-love. The myth of Narcissus provides all of us a great lesson. We do not want to fall in love with perceptions, whether ours or others'.

112

This mode of perceiving the world as you think you are perceived is unhealthy and an example of pathologic narcissism. We must love ourselves to be the best that we can be, but loving ourselves is very different than loving the image of ourself.

When we honor what is in our heart and not choose what is laid out for us by others, we are loving ourself. We are following our own path, like Bill Gates. Self-love and the pursuit of our dream is a selfish experience, but not an unhealthy one. We call this healthy narcissism. The dedication and effort required to achieve the highest level in business, arts, or sports requires healthy selfishness.

Beth Heiden Reid won a world championship in both cycling and speed skating and even made the United States Cross Country Ski Team. She unequivocally meets the definition of a great performer. And yet at the 1980 Olympics, she was pushed to tears by the media's constant critical questioning about why she did not win a gold medal and only a bronze. She responded on national TV by saying, "I'm happiest when I skate for myself. But this year I feel I have had to skate for the press. The hell with you guys."

Beth instinctively knew that a great athlete gets in the Zone for the simple joy of the experience. Some people, in Beth's case the press, thought she was letting Team USA down by being selfish and only wanting to skate for herself, but being in the Zone is a private experience. You can do it on a public stage, and others can enjoy the beauty of your performance, but you cannot get in the Zone if you care about what everyone else thinks. You must have a healthy degree of selfishness and self-love. This knowledge is imperative for achieving peak performance.

FINDING SUCCESS ONLY TO LOSE YOUR WAY

Paradoxically, pathological self-love, the need to always be the center of attention, like our mythical figure Narcissus, keeps you from the Zone. An example that illustrates this phenomenon comes from a young athlete I helped. Blake was a very good high school basketball player and, more important, he was highly motivated to be the best. His coaches told him that he could get a scholarship to a university or even go pro. But when he began to respond to the pressure of others' expectations, his goals started to shift away from pure fun to something more. He started to identify himself as being a high school star. His friends related to him in a different way. He started to see himself through the eyes of others, and suddenly he had more at stake if he played poorly. Unconsciously he felt, "If I lose, I will no longer be a high school star." One time he even referred to himself as "a teenage idol." He was clearly getting hooked on all the attention that goes with the role. Unfortunately, this process of seeking attention from others started to separate him from his ability to directly experience basketball in the pure sense.

Blake's ego-involvement created a new motivation, a less powerful form than his love of basketball. His drive to be the best gave way to his drive to satisfy his ego. He became seduced by the hype. Regardless, his talent was so pure that he continued to excel and graduated college signing a professional contract. He became rich and reached his new perceived goal of being famous. Inevitably, he had some bad days and played poorly. The coaches and media criticized him, and he took what they said to heart. He stopped believing in himself. He became vulnerable when he lost touch with the game he loved, and his motivation was usurped by the industry of professional basketball.

Ironically, but not surprisingly, the more invested he became in the response of his fans and the media, the more his confidence eroded, and Blake's career was soon over.

When Blake came to me, he was in his middle twenties and, after sharing his story, he wanted to know what had happened and why. Basketball was no longer fun for him; instead, it had been reduced to a pressure-packed work environment that was not compatible with his fragile ego. The nature of playing basketball changed for Blake when he stopped playing for himself and his dream.

Another similar example comes from the world of music. Tyler is a young man who grew up poor and shy, but had a tremendous work ethic and gift for music. He loved his music and it made him feel good to create it. For Tyler, music was fun—it was not work, it was his passion. His motivation and drive to excel were boundless. As time passed, his fortitude was repeatedly tested because his peers and parents told him that he could never make a living being an artist.

However, Tyler took a big chance and through a series of synchronistic events met a producer who got him a recording contract. The producer said that his music had a strange, ethereal quality he had not heard before, and signed him. Amazingly, his first recording became a hit and his life was transformed.

But then Tyler began partying with the celebrities, attracting all sorts of Hollywood types, and soon money, power, and some fame followed. His behavior started to change when he looked forward to being the center of attention. In a way we could metaphorically say that he started to fall in love with his own reflection. He was convinced he was going to be music's next big thing. Insidiously, he became obsessed with the Hollywood scene and lifestyle—it consumed him. His work ethic suffered terribly and he became increasingly arrogant and detached, and his passion for music evaporated.

Soon thereafter the honeymoon period was over; his record company pressured him to create more music, but it had become stale. He began to stall and could not resurrect the motivation he once had. The pressure of everyone's expectations overwhelmed him. His money began to run out, his friends became scarce, and he spiraled deep into a world of drugs.

I met Tyler when he hit this low point and was a resident of a drug rehab facility in San Diego County. It was clear to both of us that he had lost his way. His raw talent and pure motivation had led to his remarkable success. But he was seduced by the lifestyle and it became more important to him to be cool than to just be himself. He transitioned from making music for himself to making music for money and status. He fell victim to what I call the "E channel syndrome"—the pursuit of celebrity.

This innate human vulnerability to desire fame and fortune caused tremendous pain for this young man, but it has also allowed him to see the world with a clearer lens. He is now working on being mentally and physically healthy, and he has lost his obsession with being more than a one-hit wonder.

Last I heard, a sober Tyler was creating his music day and night, and another well-known music producer who courted him in his prime dropped by and was blown away by his unique sound. No surprise—maybe he never lost his way. He only misplaced it.

Blake and Tyler are examples of how success, if not kept in perspective, can contaminate pure motivation. Their obsession with fortune and fame is typical of the material world we live in today. Not staying close to their original source of inspiration was ultimately the origin of their demise. So many people are unhappy because they think wealth will give them peace. It is nice to be wealthy because wealth can allow us to have choices and freedom. But what is the healthy balance? If we work at something that is lucrative but do not enjoy the task, our motivation can still remain strong. However, if it is only the money we seek rather than the freedom it provides, our motivation is inherently compromised and we run the risk of creating a dangerous self-perpetuating cycle where the more we make, the more we spend, and we create "golden hand-cuffs" and restrict our freedom.

This innate drive to follow your heart lives within all of us. Sometimes we lose our way, like Tyler and Blake. However, we must remember that children naturally follow their heart; it is an inborn instinct. If you want to find the Zone of life, you can seek to find what makes you happy, and when you do this, your ego does not matter.

LEARN TO FIND PURE MOTIVATION

In 1999, David Duval eclipsed Tiger Woods to become the number one golfer in the world. After the tournament, David was interviewed and asked if beating Tiger motivated him. Paradoxically, he said, "I've never played to be number one in the word. I've always done it to see how good I could be and how much I could master the act of hitting a golf ball. How Tiger played has nothing to do with it."

The simple question you must ask yourself repeatedly is, "Why do I do what I do?" You need to stay attached and clear about the motivation behind your efforts.

If your motivation is for reasons of fame and fortune, it will be hard to find peak performance. If you used to love what you do and now find that your motivation is moving from intrinsic (love) to extrinsic (money), you should pause, breathe, and stop the cycle of burnout. Try to remember how it was when you started and see if you can re-create the same enthusiasm. Take a moment and think of our musician Tyler, who finally found what he thought he'd lost, but was in fact only misplaced. Ask yourself, are you like the LPGA golfer who cares too much about what others think?

Make an effort to care about the things you used to care about and note what was most important when you had the most fun. Simplify the things that have become complex. Metaphorically, see the forest from the trees. Remember, you may not be able to please everyone, but regardless, you must absolutely please yourself—like Beth Heiden Reid. Keeping your motivation pure isn't rocket science. The answer always lives within your heart. But you must stay grounded throughout the journey to access this knowledge. If you do this, you will find that the rewards are enormous—just ask a computer nerd named Bill.

ACCEPTANCE
AND FAITH
CONQUER FEAR

Our deepest fear is not that we are inadequate.
Our deepest fear is that we are powerful
beyond measure. It is our Light, not
our Darkness, that most frightens us.

—MARIANNE WILLIAMSON

F ear is the first natural enemy of the great competitor. How does Lance Armstrong reach speeds up to 60 miles an hour and stay within inches of other riders as they race down the treacherous slopes of the Pyrenees Mountains? How did Jimmy Shea careen, headfirst and at 100 miles an hour, down a steeply pitched ice-laden Skeleton track to win an Olympic gold? They conquered their fear. And though this may not be easy, it is possible. Conquering fear and accessing faith boost our ability to get in and stay in the Zone.

THE EVOLUTION OF FEAR

Great athletes must free themselves of the potentially paralytic effect of fear, but how? Fear is a universal emotion that has developed through evolution to help propagate human life. When we are fearful and in a fight-or-flight response, we are more on guard, less naïve, more motivated, hyper-alert, and physiologically stronger. We become more equipped to handle a dangerous attack from a saber-toothed tiger. This relationship between fear and survival has developed over millions of years of evolution, and in more primitive times fear served us well in maximizing our survival. In order to insure survival, fear has been imprinted within the neural circuits of the human psyche.

Yet one of fear's characteristics is that when engaged, it often becomes the master of our thoughts and behaviors, dictating an immediate fight-or-flight response. This occurs because in prehistoric times, primates, the mammals from which humans are thought to evolve, had to survive living among a variety of predators. For example, they had an intimate relationship with reptiles and snakes, all of which provided potential food for the other. To avoid becoming snake food, primates developed better eyesight to provide enhanced tracking ability, thus increasing their survivability. Additionally, they experienced fear, which enhanced their ability to escape when attacked by these predators. The fear that primates felt was real and appropriate because their lives were in danger.

Millions of years later, this evolutionary adaptation is still present. It makes sense to be fearful when you see the dorsal fin of a great white shark during an ocean swim. But it doesn't make sense to have the same emotional response when you are placed in the situation of shooting free throws in a basketball game or giving a talk to a group of colleagues. The shark poses a life-threatening risk, while a basketball game or giving a talk does not. To experience the same fear response, regardless of the inherent environmental danger, is not adaptive. In one case the fear is warranted: The primal man encountering a saber-toothed tiger should be afraid for his life. In the other case, the fear is a response to an exaggerated threat, such as losing a basketball game. You may rightly fear the potential disappointment of losing, but losing will never threaten your life. When we exaggerate the threat of a circumstance, we are distorting reality. This distortion is by definition neurotic. In the example above, the fear associated with missing a free throw in basketball is neurotic if it triggers a fight-or-flight response.

This overgeneralization of the expression of fear, meaning becoming unnecessarily fearful of situations that are not life-threatening, occurs underneath our conscious awareness. Our emotional brain experiences the competitive world as an all-or-nothing response. It does not gradate and differentiate degrees of danger. If an NBA basketball player misses a critical free throw, he is bummed out and maybe even some of his future market value becomes compromised. However, his life is not threatened. This overreaction or engagement of our fear response to non-life-threatening competitions is costly.

When we are afraid and in the midst of a fight-or-flight response, we often make poor decisions and physically experience lack of coordination and cognitive confusion. And yet a more encompassing by-product is that fear makes it impossible to feel free and become absorbed in the flow of life. Inappropriate fear responses are debilitating and make the quest for peak performance impossible. However, if you learn to understand the nature of your fear, you can disarm fear and master an emotion that most often masters us.

We can conquer fear by mobilizing four of our own innate abilities:

- the phenomena of behavioral desensitization, or "getting used to doing it"
- cognitive recontextualization, or "seeing the forest from the trees"
- spiritual faith, or "believing in God"
- know-mind awareness

BEHAVIORAL DESENSITIZATION, OR
"GETTING USED TO DOING IT"

The life of cyclist Lance Armstrong allows us to better understand how conquering fear is a realistic goal. I met Lance Armstrong in 1991, before he had ever won a Tour de France and before he developed testicular cancer. Lance was riding for the Motorola Team, and I was a guest at the team's hotel room during a bike-racing event in San Diego. During that day I talked with and closely observed many of the racers. Lance seemed like he was enjoying the success of his cycling career, although he had an unusual edge to his personality. His presence conveyed that he was not satisfied with being a very good cyclist. In fact, at that time he was not the best cyclist in the hotel room. Davis Phinney was the best at that time. However, there was something intriguing about Lance that set him apart from the other cyclists. My sense was that there would be much more to come from Lance, and I followed his career with piqued interest.

In retrospect, what was truly the most amazing and most interesting aspect about Lance Armstrong's now-storied accomplishment of winning the Tour de France seven consecutive times is that he did so *after* he survived cancer. One cannot help but entertain the question of whether or not the cancer actually played a part in his unparalleled success. Imagine being a young star athlete and being diagnosed with testicular cancer and concomitant brain and lung metastasis. His survival chances were at best 50-50. Lance's fear was not exaggerated. Yet, his terrifying situation actually enhanced his ability to conquer fear.

The reality of living with death desensitizes us to fear. In fact, if we live with any circumstance long enough, we acclimate. This ability to acclimate is experienced physiologically when we travel to high altitudes; our extraction of oxygen from the hemoglobin in our blood becomes more efficient. It is also experienced emotionally when we are left in a traumatic situation; the fear experienced in a war zone is greater for the newcomer than it is for the individual who has spent months or years in combat. In fact, in time, the experience of fear may dissipate, although the life-threatening situation may persist.

I am sure that Lance is no exception. He was forced to live with fear not by his design, but by destiny. In time, a chronic life-threatening stress, like cancer, causes the threshold that triggers the fear response to be higher for the fear response to be activated. The fear of losing a bike race would pale in comparison to dealing with the fear associated with radiation and chemotherapy treatment for malignant cancer. Lance's situation forced him to realize that once you are born, you are destined to die, and it is when you can accept and embrace this reality you start to conquer fear.

The human capacity for "desensitization," or simply getting used to things, is enormous and happens automatically if we allow ourselves to continue to revisit the same stressful situation. The knowledge that this happens without conscious effort is comforting and gives hope, often allowing us to persevere through difficult times.

If it is the first time you are on the big stage, it is natural to be nervous, and you can take solace that each additional experience will be easier and easier. Lance's experience may have helped him master his mind and conquer his fear.

RECONTEXTUALIZATION, OR "SEEING THE FOREST FROM THE TREES"

If your entire world is built around the sport of gymnastics, the fear of blowing the lead on the last day of the Olympics may feel similar to the fear of a primal man encountering a saber-toothed tiger. It is easier to choke when you give too much importance to your performance. We choke when we care too much about the wrong thing. Therefore, another critical element for conquering fear is to see the bigger picture, to see that whatever it is that you are competing in is only part of your life. When you see the greater context, you allow yourself to allocate the appropriate importance to your endeavor. You will care less about striking out if you have just experienced the tragic loss of a loved one. You are more likely to realize that a baseball game is not life and death, and this thought will facilitate you relaxing at the plate even if you are facing a 100-mile-per-hour fastball.

It is essential for the great performer to see the race for what it is and no more. I always like to remind golfers on the PGA Tour who become fixated on the importance of a particular putt that at least 5 billion people on this planet really don't care if you make it or miss it. This comment may seem flip, but it is really designed to help the athlete see the larger context and get out of his own head. It is imperative for him to realize that his sport is not a matter of life and death; when he manages this perspective, his mind and body will automatically relax.

Developing a larger perspective of life outside of the one you live inherently gives you the ability to be less neurotic and apply less pressure to yourself when competing. This ability to see beyond your own world and see what you are doing in the grand scheme of things inherently soothes the tense competitor and keeps fear in check.

In 1993 the great basketball coach Jimmy Valvano was a young man in his forties whose body was ridden with cancer. But before he died, he gave one of the most memorable speeches in sports history at the ESPN annual awards show that commenced the beginning of the Jimmy V Foundation for the fight against cancer. During this speech he was helped to the microphone, barely able to walk, writhing in pain as his body was riddled with metastasis cancer. He rocked the house by talking about living life to its fullest and never giving up. His "never give up" words have invigorated the spirit of millions of cancer victims.

Six years after that speech, I was working with four young golfers who were all in the final round of the Q School on the eve of securing their card the next morning. The boys were all caught up in their own action and completely self-absorbed. The tension that filled the room was palpable and not very conducive to the relaxation they needed to recharge and play their best on the big day. I asked them if they would let me show them a video and I popped in the Jimmy V speech. Fifteen minutes later the boys were moved to the verge of tears, speechless. The tension in the room had dissipated. The speech gave the boys a recontextualization of their own world. Golf was no longer life or death; it was a sport. And no matter at what level sports are played, they are designed for fun and entertainment. The next day the boys all played with tremendous poise and focus, each of them earning a PGA Tour card and achieving a lifelong dream.

When I am asked to help athletes deal with fear and anxiety, the first thing I ask them to define is their exposure, meaning, what is the worst thing that can happen? What is it that they are truly afraid of? Often I get interesting answers, such as "I don't know" or "I guess I fear losing." After making them think about this question more deeply, then their answers become less vague. A baseball player might say he fears striking out, and a salesman might say he fears not booking the account. I ask people to think of their worst scenario and how it compares to cancer or war. I ask them if they can live with it, and normally with a relieved look, they relax. It is human nature to fear fear, but it is not necessary—we have the ability to master this primal emotion, by understanding its origin.

To do this, you first need to draw upon a bigger perspective; then you must accept the possibility that you can lose. By taking these steps, you paradoxically increase the likelihood of winning. Understanding that life goes on and that you will survive no matter what happens during a performance will allow you to do your best. If you engage in these thoughts—seeing the bigger picture, understanding the worst-case scenario, and reminding yourself that life goes on—then your fear will naturally dissipate. You will perform freely and more effectively.

IT'S A QUESTION OF FAITH

Fear's most formidable opponent is less cerebral. Recontextualization (seeing the bigger picture) and desensitization (getting used to things) can disarm fear, but it is faith that kills fear. It is not a coincidence that many athletes thank God for their success. Indeed, faith is our strongest ally in the battle against fear.

In my internal medicine training at UCLA, I always dreaded seeing the terminally sick patient who was an atheist; conversely, I was relieved when the dying patient had strong religious and/or spiritual beliefs. There was always a palpable difference in the comfort level between the two individuals. Reinforcing my experience are many studies suggesting that the quality of life is better for terminal patients if they have a strong faith.

The concept of faith implies complete trust. In religious doctrines, faith implies having complete trust in God, and it is this core component that has allowed religion to serve mankind in many ways. In ancient times religions provided a framework for human behavior—teaching society morality while helping the human psyche deal with life's fragile and uncertain nature. If uncertainty coupled with a sense of pending doom defines fear, and if fear is a biologically programmed response to intense competition, then it is no surprise that faith, the feeling of complete trust, is a critical component of success in competitive environments.

However, spirituality, faith, and religious conviction are very personal and private matters. Most people believe in God, but not all. And yet we can all utilize the idea, if not the reality, of faith as a way to conquer our fear.

This power, of believing in something greater than our-selves, is not endorsed by all of us. For those who are more cynical and have a difficult time believing in a greater power, I would like to share an argument that we debated in my col-lege philosophy and physics classes. Physics, in a broad sense, is the study of nature, and the second law of thermodynamics describes the phenomena that all energy inevitably dis-charges from the system that contains it. In practical terms this means that in nature everything will ultimately disinte-grate and turn to dust. This process of energy dissipating is called the law of entropy. And there are no known exceptions except the fact that life itself does not dissipate, but rather self-perpetuates in various forms. Genetic mutation and evo-lution are mechanisms for perpetuating life on Earth.

We may think that it is we who wear the jeans, but it is the genes that wear us. In fact, we as humans have more bacterial cells in our bodies than human cells. Furthermore, we have more viral particles than bacterium. We are all an amalgamation of various life forms and forces. Life's energy, or *prana* as it is called in the ancient language of Sanskrit, is a force that keeps us alive and healthy. It exists beyond the physical laws of thermodynamics. In my personal view, I have always thought of the continual nature of life as a con-tradiction to the second law of thermodynamics and as log-ical evidence for the existence God or some higher power. Whether you believe in God or not, if you can recognize a life force, you can draw on the power of faith.

The great psychiatrist Carl Jung was once asked on national television in the late 1950s, in a high-drama moment, if he believed in God. The intellectual community and religious communities anxiously waited to hear what this great genius of their time would say. Dr. Jung told the world that he did not believe in God, and everyone gasped. He continued with an unwavering conviction, paused, and said he "knew God." His words settled a world filled with danger and uncertainty. Faith in God or some higher force allows us to feel connected and united to something greater than ourselves. Maybe we become more like what the famous Eastern philosopher Thich Nhat Hanh calls the "interbeing." He teaches us that the largest living organism in the world is a grove of Aspen trees in Colorado that all share the same root system—similar to what quantum physics has shown to be true—that we are all interconnected. And in Sun Tzu's famous text *The Art of War*, he posits that when people believe that their leader is benevolent and feel united, they fight better because they fight without fear, forgetting danger.

Faith can be many things, but at its center it is a belief that we belong to something larger than ourselves. This belief system gives us a sense of immortality that allows us to act without fear. Faith allows us to stay calm in the face of adversity. It shields us from reacting to negative emotions and thoughts. If you place faith and fear in the battleground of the human psyche, there is only one victor.

VICTORY OVER FEAR

We will always fear what we do not know. But we do have the power to get used to that which we fear. Desensitization, or getting used to things, happens automatically if we place ourself in the same environment repeatedly. In Lance's case, his experience with cancer desensitized him to fear. Recontextualization or seeing the bigger picture is a process that we can mobilize, exemplified by showing the young golfers at Q School the Jimmy V speech. And last and most important, we can lean into our faith—whether it is faith in Jesus, Allah, Buddha, Rama, the Force, or just our own natural abilities; in all its forms, faith kills fear.

BUILD CONFIDENCE AND WIN

I am, indeed, a king, because I know how to rule myself.

—PIETRO ARETINO

onfidence is the cornerstone of success in all domains of life, and developing it is much like nurturing a garden. It takes attention, gentle care, and vigilance. Poor self-confidence is like a garden that has been overgrown with weeds. The gardener must search through all the foliage to find and nurture the flowers. Self-confidence can be nurtured by many gardeners, including coaches, family, and mentors. But it is most important that you understand how to nurture and develop your own self-confidence.

When you grow confident, you are essentially learning specific concrete knowledge that bonds your intention with your ability, thus forming trust. It is this trust or confidence that forms a crucial bridge to being Zone-like—in your attitude, your approach, and your ability to realize your goals and turn your desire into will.

THE SCIENCE OF CONFIDENCE

Though little known outside of academia, self-confidence has been shown to be a concrete, achievable goal supported by science. Dr. Albert Bandura, Professor Emeritus at Stanford University, developed the field of "self-efficacy." Dr. Bandura's principles sit at the core of building your confidence. His research shows that there are four essential components of confidence.

The first are called mastery experiences, where you have the past experience of doing well. Take baseball, for example. If a hitter hits a home run in his last at bat, he logically sets the stage to be more confident in future at bats. The second component is called vicarious learning. If a child watches her neighbors jump into the local pool, she may think she can do it, too. Vicarious learning comes from seeing someone do something that you can see yourself doing as well. The third is by modeling someone's behavior that inspires you to achieve your goal. Remember the old

Gatorade commercial featuring Michael Jordan? The slogan "Be like Mike" was carefully crafted to subliminally couple drinking Gatorade with being a confident champion. The last ingredient of self-confidence is social persuasion, or receiving positive verbal reinforcement from someone you trust. Think of the first time you went skiing and your father took you up the chairlift. Anxiously looking down the slope, trying to find enough confidence, you heard your father's encouragement, giving you the courage to go for it. This is an example of verbal persuasion.

I had the pleasure of witnessing a wonderful example of learning and integrating these four components of self-confidence with the meteoric rise of the PGA player Rich Beem. In 1998, Rich Beem was selling cell phones. At that time Paul Stankowski, a peer from college golf, won on both the Nationwide and PGA Tour. Beemer felt that if Paul could do it, he could—vicarious learning in a nutshell. The next year Beem followed suit. He qualified for the PGA Tour and won the Kemper Open. His mastery experience of winning further enhanced his confidence and he won again in 2002 at the International. Beemer was not done yet. The very next week, brimming with confidence, he found himself on the final nine hole of the last major championship of the year, being chased by Tiger Woods. His caddie, Billy Heim, kept telling him he could do it, helping to reinforce Beemer's confidence. And, as Rich later told me, "I knew that if I kept hitting the shots I could hit,

Tiger would not catch me." That day Rich Beem beat Tiger Woods down the final stretch of a major championship and became the PGA champion. His whole life was transformed.

However, it's not enough to know the four components to access the Zone; you also have to know how to mobilize these concepts and integrate them into your experience to nurture your confidence.

BECOMING A DOCTOR

I always wanted to become a doctor, and throughout my youth I never thought it would be possible. The energy of my youth was focused on being a table tennis player. My grades were poor throughout high school and my attendance was worse. My family, with good reason, thought I wasn't doctor material.

After I finished my professional table tennis career, I pondered the question of whether or not I should—or could—go to college. Deep in my heart I always longed to become a doctor, but with my academic track record I knew that it was as unlikely as winning the lottery.

However, good fortune smiled, when my mother told me that Rice University, in Houston, Texas, where my parents were then living, had a 5 percent rule, where they took applicants with unusual backgrounds. I asked her what mine was, and she said, "Your Ping-Pong." I smiled, thinking that this was the first time my mother had ever had anything even modestly positive to say about hitting the little white celluloid ball.

Rice's policy, coupled with my mother's chutzpa, personally pleading with the admissions office to admit her son, resulted in my acceptance to a very rigorous academic university—a terribly frightening realization for someone who rarely attended high school.

The university's policy was to start freshmen like me off on academic probation, knowing that we were a high-risk group. I remember my parents calling me and encouraging me to hang in while covertly anticipating my failure. Equally as nervous, I took the attitude that I take when I gamble in Vegas: Last as long as they let you play. I started my first semester and decided to give it my best shot. Throughout that first year I kept my nose to the grindstone and, lo and behold, I made good grades, and my dream of being a psychiatrist was reawakened. In fact, at the end of the first year, I surprised myself and managed a 4.0 GPA and experienced my first *mastery experience.* My confidence started to take on a life of its own. After that semester, I transferred to Stanford University, a school where there were many more students, many of whom were also former athletes, like myself. I knew I would feel more at home at this new school.

At Stanford the volume was turned up. I felt like a much smaller fish in a much bigger pond. But I felt that if I studied hard, learned the material to the best of my ability, and performed well on the tests, I would be successful—no matter what grade resulted. I was focused in the moment, not in the future. After completing a second year of college, my friends and I used to joke about the upperclassmen who got into medical school, remarking that if they could do it, we could. We spent a lot of time in the library studying with them, and in time felt for the most part that we had what they had. I knew if these nerds, as my friends and I called them, could do it, I could. This experience of vicariously seeing myself able to achieve my goal by seeing others do it further enhanced my confidence.

When it came time to make a decision to apply to medical school, I was filled with self-doubt once again. Stanford was one thing, and I knew medical school was another. I was well aware that intense dedication would be needed as well as massive memorization of facts and inhumane hours working in the hospital. The whole process seemed infinitely too intimidating for a rehabilitated Ping-Pong player like me. Nevertheless, my friends persuaded me to believe that I could make a good score on the medical school entrance exam (MCATs) and achieve my dream. It was not long before they made me a believer, a believer in my own ability to become a doctor. I decided to study hard for the MCATs and finally had the confidence to go for it. I had unknowingly just experienced social persuasion, which had boosted my confidence. After being rejected by eight consecutive medical schools, I received the one letter that changed my life: I was accepted to the University of Texas.

The next year was not easy, and after a stressful and unsuccessful time sweating in the Houston humidity, I quit medical school in a funk of shattered confidence. I did some soul-searching and went back to northern California to work at a hospital in the psychiatric ward as a psych tech, essentially the lowest-level job. I loved it because I had the opportunity to spend a great deal of time with the patients, whom I thoroughly enjoyed. However, my favorite person was a professor, Dr. David Spiegel, now the associate chairman of psychiatry at Stanford University, a renowned psychiatrist and one cool dude. I loved that when he came through, everyone stopped and listened to whatever he had to say. Working near Dr. Spiegel, I slowly, started to feel better about myself, and at year's end I returned to medical school at the University of Texas. There, I began to actively model Dr. Spiegel's career, reading all his journal articles and going to hear him speak whenever possible. I felt comforted with the knowledge that being a psychiatrist, working in sports, and studying the Zone was not so much something I wanted to do, but was rather something I would do simply because it was a feeling deep within me. I had unknowingly mobilized the four components of self-confidence and, in turn, had nurtured my own confidence.

CREATING YOUR OWN GARDEN OF CONFIDENCE

You can grow your own self-confidence by mobilizing the four components.

Mastery experiences provide the cornerstone of confidence, but they are nurtured by paying careful attention to process goals and not results. If you do well and don't win, you can still have a mastery experience if you keep the attitude that your goal was to play well. If you do your best in both preparation and actual performance, no one can consider you a failure. Keep a record of your past experiences in a journal.

You should also look around and surround yourself with the most talented people, people who have already achieved what you want. Never be afraid to ask questions and learn. There is no such thing as a stupid question. Never be afraid to ask the best player for a match. You may surprisingly find something that John McEnroe found when he first played Jimmy Connors—that you are better than you thought you were, and your confidence builds with this knowledge. This process of vicariously learning is accessible to everyone; indeed, it is part of human nature. Look to see if there are friends or associates who have accomplished what you seek, and observe to see if you can do what they did. If you think you can, make note of it.

Spend time with positive people, people who will

encourage you to seek your dream and inspire you to find the inner strength needed. Negative people are not necessary. It is your responsibility and choice to create environments of positive thought. Surround yourself with successful and positive people and let them persuade you that you can reach your goal—thus fostering the Zone-enhancing tool of verbal persuasion.

And, identify who it is that inspires you and learn everything you can about them. Model his or her work ethic as an approach to life, and soon enough you will find that your garden of confidence has just grown. Identify who it is that inspires you and seek them out.

If you do these four things in sports, business, or some aspect of your personal life, your confidence will grow, and you in turn will have developed tangible evidence that you can, and have, an ability to make your dreams real. Turn your desire into will, build your confidence, and make the Zone a reality.

PERFORM UNDER PRESSURE

A better life habit is to respond
with performance preparation which
is geared to playing under pressure.
Playing under pressure is not to be feared,
it is merely the normal circumstance of performing.

—OLIVER STEINER, VIOLINIST

All who have achieved great success in their field—
whether in athletics, art, drama, business, academics,
or science—have one thing in common: At their core, they
are all great competitors. They share the ability to shine
under the most intense pressure, and make it look easy.
They are able to put aside the frenzy of emotional, psychological, and physical stresses and rise above them. What is
their gift and how do they do it? We all live in a highly
competitive world where winning is everything and

coming in second gets you a pat on the back. Can anyone name the runner-up at the last Tour de France or the runner-up at the last World Series? Or who was short-listed for the Nobel Prize or Academy Award? Probably not. So how can we learn to think like the great champions and model their mind-set so we, too, can thrive in competition and get into the Zone of life?

This question presents a formidable challenge, yet the answer is paradoxically simple.

It is often said that athletes "choke" when they care too much. This is not true. All humans, including great athletes, choke. It is okay to choke. It is part of human nature to, at times, feel the pressure of the moment and not perform your best. However, we perform best under pressure when we minimize the choke factor, and the best way to do this is to care about the right things and not the wrong things. For example, worrying profusely about some future result is one of the wrong things. The great competitors care as much as anyone, however, they care in a more intelligent and effective way. They know instinctively that sport and competition are meant to be fun and that when we lose our sense of fun we cannot excel. The right way to care is not to care less, but to develop a healthy and playful attitude toward competition, regardless of circumstance.

Take for example an experience I had several years ago caddying for my brother at the AT&T Pebble Beach National Pro-Am. All three days my brother's amateur partner was San Francisco 49er NFL three-time Pro Bowl lineman Harris Barton. During those days and the dinners that followed, my brother and I spent a lot of time with Harris. But what left an indelible impression on me is the one night our two families were at dinner together and my brother embarrassed me and told Harris I was a huge fan of the 49ers, in particular their Hall of Fame quarterback Joe Montana.

I was embarrassed because it was true: My fascination with Joe started early in my college days when his red Ferrari would blaze by the trailer I lived in on Sand Hill Road in Woodside, California.

I understood that Joe was neither exceptionally fast nor strong as a player. And yet he was, in my view, the definition of a true winner, having engineered thirty-one fourth-quarter comebacks and four Super Bowl victories. He never seemed to crumble under pressure and possessed that intangible mental quality that defines the greatest athletes.

One night at dinner, after a couple of glasses of Harris's best red wine, Harris started to talk about Joe. He began by telling us a story about the last game of his rookie season, and to paraphrase him, he said, "In 1989, we were in the Super Bowl against the Cincinnati Bengals and were losing with only three minutes to play. On our own eight yard line in the huddle, we were waiting for Montana to give us the play; we were so nervous we could hardly breathe, and I could hear my heart beating. We were all worried about the next three minutes and we looked like deer in headlights." Harris paused and looked up. "We knew we needed a miracle to win, and our nerves were getting the best of us.

"Joe stepped into the huddle and blew our minds. He did not immediately call the play; in fact, he said, 'Hey, boys, do you see John Candy sitting in the stands? He's near the exit ramp.'"

Harris continued the story, "And right there in that moment, suddenly, our fear, like smoke in the aftermath of an explosion, dissipated. The whole vibe in the huddle changed, and Joe looked up and gave us the play." Loose as a goose, twinkle in his eye, the ever-intense "Joe Cool" rallied his team, completing eight of nine passes and scoring the final touchdown with only seconds left, winning Super Bowl XXIII.

So why did Harris tell us eager listeners this story about Montana's comments that led his team to victory? How is it that a seemingly irrelevant observation noting the whereabouts of the famous comedic actor, in the final seconds of a Super Bowl, provides insight into the mind of arguably one of the best clutch quarterbacks in history? The nature of the Montana's comment is not only simple, it is genius. It provides a wonderful example of how humor dissipates nervous energy and allows us to focus on the task at hand. The players in the huddle, especially the young ones, like Harris Barton, were exceptionally nervous, something that was evident to Joe. When Montana asked everyone to shift their

attention to John Candy, the team unknowingly partici-
pated in a Zone-enhancing tool that relaxed the mind—a
brief attentional shift strategy coupled with the image of
something funny. Just imagine you are in the huddle, choking under the pressure, awaiting your leader to call the next
play, and instead he asks you and everyone else to look over
at a jolly, overweight famous comedian. For that moment
your mind's focus releases and relaxes, allowing the pressure to dissipate and providing time to regroup.

Similarly, when faced with a public speaking situation,
we have all heard the commonly given advice to "imagine
that everyone is naked." This advice may not always be
practical or realistic, but the concept conveys a fundamental truth. Don't take yourself too seriously, find some levity
and humor in the situation, and you will survive the competition.

Another example of humor facilitating survival in
intense situations is from the Academy Award–winning
movie *Life Is Beautiful*, where the protagonist is played by
Roberto Benigni. He uses humor to help the Italian Jewish
children deal with stress of being imprisoned in a German
concentration camp. In this incredibly creative way,
Benigni makes the children smile and laugh when he interprets (really misinterprets) the Nazi captain's German into
Italian during very tense group meetings where many of
the children are directed to the gas chambers. Although
terribly disturbing, this is a wonderfully powerful example

of how introducing humor into the most stressful situations promotes survival. Humor inherently disarms the experience of stress.

In the classic text *The Ego and the Mechanisms of Defense*, written by Anna Freud, Sigmund's daughter, she wrote about how the mind copes with stress. She described a spectrum of coping skills, ranging from the maladaptive to the most adaptive, humor being among them. Humor and self-parody (the ability to make fun of yourself) give us the room to be human and make mistakes, subtly giving us a sense of freedom that translates into unhindered performance—similar to children playing in the Zone.

The Zone cannot be forced or controlled. It organically evolves from creating the optimal environment. It is as if the nature of the Zone has a life of its own. It is an inexplicable phenomenon. We can move in and out of it, and it can happen in degrees. Falling into the Zone is not that different from falling in love. They both come out of nowhere. They both can dissipate in a moment's notice, and without passion they cease to survive. The key to staying in the Zone requires a receptive and playful attitude while simultaneously being impeccably prepared. Sport is an experience to be enjoyed and not feared. And life is a sport.

Getting into the Zone is less about what you do in the moment; it is more about what is done long before the competition. The overarching goal is to develop a mastery of your mind, like the samurai swordsman. Joe Montana exemplifies how a playful attitude thrives under pressure. However, Joe's unique ability to have fun competing while being under intense scrutiny was predicated by his tremendous perseverance and commitment. Joe was always impeccably prepared for each game, and this is why he was able to play with the passion of the unencumbered mind. Great champions invest the extra energy in being fully prepared, and that is why they can relax on game day and have a little fun. They intuitively understand the physics concept of "activation energy."

Activation energy is the energy required to start a chemical reaction. For example, you may not know that paper burns at 451 degrees Fahrenheit and does not ignite at 450 degrees. Now imagine yourself lost in a forest, cold, needing warmth. You invest energy by rubbing two sticks together, causing friction in hope of igniting some paper and leaves. You create heat by your efforts and even raise the friction area's temperature up to 450 degrees without successfully creating fire. Sadly, you quit in discouragement, not knowing that the activation energy is 451 degrees. However, if you push a little harder and create a little more heat and raise the temperature one degree, the chain reaction occurs and the fire ignites—burning without more effort, burning by itself.

Great champions know that if they push a little more and prepare better than their competitors, they will move past the threshold and consequently set the stage to enter into the Zone. The difference between good and great is immeasurably small. Sometimes all it takes is a bit more perseverance and you find yourself at the next level. This process of giving that little extra builds upon itself and forms the foundation for great performances.

Do not take the path of least resistance. It will not lead to transformation and your life will not change. Without change, life is mundane, often leaving us living vicariously through others, wasting precious time. Take a stand, allow yourself to dream but realize that there are no shortcuts.

You cannot buy the Zone. The Zone is not for sale for $19.99 or any price: It's free. Indeed, the Zone is within you.

So what do these great athletes show us? Are they truly different from you and me? The answer is, they are not. We are all made of the same genetic protoplasm, as are our heroes. We all have the same evolutionary hardware. However, they have programmed their minds to believe in themselves, and they hang tough when the chips are down. They mobilize the ten fundamentals without exception and mold them into one. These athletes and exceptional people in other disciplines distinctively know that the difference between success and failure is paper thin. It is this knowledge that drives them to create enough activation energy to transform themselves, and achieve self-actualization and often greatness.

So turn off the TV. Dream of your hero—whether he or

she is Bill Gates, Joe Montana, Eleanor Roosevelt, or the Dalai Lama. But don't live vicariously through them. Let them inspire you.

You do not have to search far and wide to find the Zone. Embrace what is already inside of you. The more we engage in doing whatever it is that brings us passion, the richer our life experience becomes. To recognize that we can live in the Zone is as natural as recognizing that all children have the capacity to have fun when they play.

Realizing and creating one's own destiny is not only for the "rich and famous." It is a God-given right for all of us. It is no different from children playing in the Zone. All we have to do is to start the chain reaction and play.

So, the next time you find yourself in the heat of battle, whether on the golf course or in the midst of an important presentation, think of these interlocking fundamentals: Let the competitive juices flow in your brain, take a second to pause, and imagine John Candy smiling in the corner of the room. Have fun—life is a sport—play, and the Zone will be yours.

ACKNOWLEDGMENTS

I am grateful to many people for their insightful and inspirational help and guidance throughout the process of writing this book. First, I would like to thank my editor at Perigee, Meg Leder, whose thoughtful reading of my work has been invaluable; my agent, Farley Chase, for his wise counsel; and Billie Fitzpatrick, my collaborator and whose vision, skill, and unwavering support has provided the foundation for this project.

In addition, many athletes shared their stories and their experiences, all of which fueled the fire in this book, including Rich Beem, David Duval, Joel Kribel, Craig Lile, Billy Casper, Eric Heiden, John McEnroe, Brad Lardon, Brenda Taylor, Samantha Magee, Jimmy Shea, Dave Binn, Perry Schwartzberg, Steve Holcomb, Billy Heim, and David Leadbetter.

My medical colleagues and friends who have also been very important and valuable, sharing their insight and expertise, including the late Chris Gillin, M.D., Bob Niculescu, M.D., James Lohr, M.D., John Polich, Ph.D., Carlton Perry, M.D., David Bergman, M.D., Michael Fitzgerald, M.D., Sian Beilock, Ph.D., and Jim Bauman, Ph.D.

I would also like to thank my very dear friends for their patience and immeasurable support: Marty Bauer, Jens Fellke, Dave Watt, Tom Strong, Richard Bunt, Chris McGirr, and Jon Schulberg.

And last but certainly not least, I would like to thank my family, whose love and belief in me have been a great source of strength and encouragement: my wife, Nadine Lardon, Psy.D.; my father, Robert T. Lardon (aka Sweet Swinger); my mother, Barbara Lardon; my sister-in-law, Sabine Schoenberg; my brother, Robert V. Lardon; and my daughters, Alexis and Lindsay.

INDEX

Academy Award, 146, 149
Accenture Match Play Championship, 49
activation energy, 151–52
Addams, Jane, 10
Agassi, André, 7
Allen, Woody, 89–90
anxiety, effects of
    anxiogenic activity, 71
    comprehensive training, 24
    controlling and regulating, 24, 71–72
    on dreams, 7–8
    on focus, 67, 69–72
    on performance, 16–17, 19,
        22–23
    optimal performance zone, 23
    physiologic hyper-arousal, 23
    total preparation, 24–25
    worst-case scenario, 129–30
anxiogenic activity, 71
Aretino, Pietro, 135
Armstrong, Lance, 121, 125–27, 134
The Art of War (Sun Tzu), 15, 16, 133
attentional shift, 97–99, 149
attention deficit disorder (ADD),
    74–75
AT&T Pebble Beach National Pro-Am,
    146–47
automation, 20–24

bacterium, 132
Bandura, Albert, 136
Barton, Harris, 147–49
basics, getting back to (Marc, the
    stockbroker), 54–60
Bauman, James, 93
Beem, Rich, 65, 96, 137–38
behavioral desensitization (getting used
    to it), 125–27
"Be like Mike" slogan (Gatorade), 137
Belock, Sian, 48–49
Benigni, Roberto, 149
Berra, Yoga, 99
Binn, Dave, 92, 101
Bob Hope Classic, 61
Bonaparte, Napoleon, 103
brain, 47
    attention deficit disorder (ADD),
        74–75
    body and, bidirectional relationship
        between, 98–99
    conscious awareness (just doing it),
        50–51
    highway hypnosis, 72–73
    instincts, 47–48
    mild distortion, 89–90
    negative and extraneous thoughts,
        50–51

brain (*cont.*)
  neurosis, 89
  overthinking (keeping it simple),
    48–50
  psychosis, 89
  split-mind trance ability, 72–74, 75
  Tiger trance, 72–74
  see also effort and trust, balance
    between; emotions and thoughts
breathing techniques, 98
British Open, 67
Buddhism, 30

cancer
  Armstrong, 121, 125–27, 134
  death, reality of living with, 125–26
  Valvano, 128–29, 134
Candy, John, 148–49, 153
Casper, Billy, 61–62
catastrophizing, 90–92
Chang, Michael, 7
childbirth, 33–34
choke factor, 146
  see also pressure
Cincinnati Bengals, 147–48
competition
  activation energy, 151–52
  choke factor, 146
  complete trust, 131
  going from practice range to,
    15–16
  humor, minimizing with, 145–51
  thriving during, 99–100
Computer Center Corporation, 105
confidence, 135–36
  components of, 136
    learning and integrating,
      examples of, 136–41
    mastery experiences, 136, 139, 142
    modeling behavior, 136–37, 141,
      143
    social persuasion, 137, 140–41,
      142–43
    vicarious learning, 136, 140, 142
  creating, 142–43

Connors, Jimmy, 6, 142
conscious awareness (just doing it), 50–51
controllable/noncontrollable variables,
    76–79, 82–84
creativity, 5, 11, 64
Cruise, Tom, 109
crunch time, 76
crystal methamphetamine, 35–36

Dalai Lama, 153
daydreaming, 4
death, reality of living with, 125–30
depression, 35–38
desensitization (getting used to it),
    125–27, 134
desire
  defining, 30–31
  transforming into will (*see* will)
direct experience, 53, 66–67, 67
displacement goggles, 51–52
distractions, 65–67
dopamine, 35–36
dreams, 1–2
  accessing (exercise), 11–13
  daydreaming, 4
  discovering knowledge, 3–5
  lucid, 5, 12
  real, 2–3
  trusting and believing in, 5–11
drug addiction, 35–38
Duval, David, 66, 118–19

E channel syndrome, 117
effort and trust, balance between
  conscious awareness and (just doing
    it), 50–51
  displacement goggles, 51–52
  getting back to the basics, homework
    for, 54–60
  keeping it simple, 60–64
  stressing out, 52–53
ego, 9–10
  involvement (losing your way), 114–18
  observing (*see* know-mind awareness)
  superego, 9–10

The Ego and the Mechanisms of Defense
    (A. Freud), 150
Einstein, Albert, 4, 10
Eisenhower, Dwight D., 61
Elkington, Steve, 96–97, 101
emotions and thoughts, 85–86
    catastrophizing, 90–92
    differentiating ourselves from, 88,
        96–97
    neurotic continuum, 86–90
    pain and anger, example of (Jimmy
        Shea), 93–96
    thought substitution, 96–97
    thriving during competition, 99–100
    see also know-mind awareness;
        visualization
ESPN annual awards show, 128–29, 134
extrinsic motivation, 104–6, 112

faith, 130–33, 134
fear, 121–22
    death, reality of living with, 125–30
    desensitization (getting used to it),
        125–27, 134
    evolution of, 122–24
    faith, 130–33, 134
    fight-or-flight response, 122–24
    as motivator, 112
    recontextualization (seeing the forest
        from the trees), 127–30, 134
    victory over, 134
fight-or-flight response, 122–24
focus
    attention deficit disorder (ADD),
        74–75
    children at play, 68–69
    controllable/noncontrollable
        variables, 76–79, 82–84
    direct experience, 66–67
    energy, 69
    exercise in (two scorecards),
        79–82
    media attention, 65–66
    monkey mind, 67–68

    trance, 72–74
    on what is in front of you, 70–72
Fortune 500 companies, 34
Freud, Anna, 150
Frost, Robert, 105
fun, 68–69

Galloway, Timothy, 62
Gates, Bill, 105–6, 113, 119, 153
Gatorade, 137
genes, 132
Gerulaitis, Vitas, 6
goals, 76
God, 131–33
Gonzales, Pancho, 97, 100
greatness, 24–25

Haney, Hank, 65
Harmon, Claude, 74
Harvard University, 31, 105–6
Heiden, Eric, 32–33, 40–43
Heim, Billy, 96–97, 137–38
hierarchy of needs, 10–11
highway hypnosis, 72–73
Hopi Indians, 3
humor, minimizing pressure with, 145–51
hyper-arousal, 23

id, 9–10
imperturbable composure, 99
The Inner Game of Tennis (Galloway), 62
instincts, 47–48, 60–61, 118
interbeing, 133
International Tournament, 137
intrinsic motivation, 104–6, 112

James, William, 31
Jimmy V Foundation, 129
Jordan, Michael, 137
Jung, Carl, 133
"Just do it" slogan (Nike), 50

Kekule, Friedrich, 4
Kemper Open, 137

know-mind awareness
  basis of, 100
  developing, 97–99
  explained, 87–88
  rules for, 100–102
  separating from yourself, 100

Lardon, Brad, 19, 146–47
Last Samurai (film), 109
law of entropy, 132
Life Is Beautiful (film), 149–50
Lile, Craig, 19, 20
LPGA, 110, 111, 119
lucid dreams, 5, 12

Magee, Sam (Samantha), 49–50
Man on Fire (film), 24
Marc, the stockbroker, 54–60
Maslow, Abraham, 10
Masters Golf Tournament, 17, 74
mastery experiences, 136, 139, 142
McEnroe, John, 6–7, 142
Medical school entrance exam
    (MCATs), 140
Medina Golf Club, 65
meditation, 90
Mickelson, Phil, 17–18, 26, 107
Microsoft, 106
mild distortion, 89–90
modeling behavior, 136–37, 141, 143
monkey mind, 67–68
Montana, Joe, 147–49, 150–51, 153
Mother Teresa, 29
motivation, 103–4, 112–14
  ego-involvement (losing your way),
      114–18
  fame vs. the best you can be,
      106–10
  fear-based, 112
  finding, 118–19
  healthy narcissism, 112–14
  intrinsic vs. extrinsic, 104–6, 112
  playing for someone else, 110–11
  pure, defined, 112

napping, 17–20
narcissism, 112–13
  healthy, 112–14
narcissistic, defined, 112
Narcissus, 112, 114
National Junior Table Tennis
    Championship, 97
Nationwide Tour, 19, 137
NBA, 124
negative and extraneous thoughts, 50–51
neurosis, 89
neurotic continuum, 86–90
NFL, 92, 147
Nhat Hanh, Thich, 133
Nicklaus, Jack, 18, 59, 60
Nike, 50
Nobel Prize, 146
noisy mind, 67–68

Oakland Hills Country Club, 48
objective reality, 88–89
Olympics
  Cross Country Ski Team, 113
  Oath, 93
  Shea, 93–95
  Team USA, 49–50, 113
  U.S. Training Center, 93
optimal performance zone, 23
overthinking (keeping it simple),
    48–50

pain and anger, example of (Jimmy Shea),
    93–96
Peltz, Dave, 17
performance, peak
  anxiety, effects on, 16–17, 19, 22–23
  facilitating, 72, 76–79
  healthy narcissism, 113–14
  optimal performance zone, 23
  reality distortion, 90
PGA Championship, 65, 137–38
PGA Tour
  AT&T Pebble Beach National
      Pro-Am, 146–47

Beem's victory over Woods, 137–38
Bob Hope Classic, 61
British Open, 67
Casper, 61–62
going from practice range to
    competition, 15–16
International, 137
Kemper Open, 137
Masters Golf Tournament, 17, 74
Nationwide Tour, 19, 137
peak performance, facilitating,
    76–77
PGA Championship, 65, 137–38
Qualifying School, 19–20, 129, 134
Senior, 107
Sony Open, 20
Stankowski, 137
two scorecards exercise, 79–82
U.S. Open Golf Championship,
    96–97
Phinney, Davis, 125
physics, 132, 133
play, 68–69
polio vaccine, 4, 5, 25–26
posture, 98
prana, 132
preferential pathways, 50
preparation
    as a building block, 26–27
    training, 24–26
preshot routine, 48–49
pressure
    activation energy, 151–52
    humor, minimizing with, 145–51
Price, Nick, 66
problem solving, 5
process-oriented thinking, 77
psychosis, 89
public speaking situations, 149
pursuit of celebrity, 117

Q School (PGA Qualifying School),
    19–20, 129, 134
quantum physics, 133

reality continuum, 89
reality distortion, 90
recontextualization (seeing the forest from
    the trees), 127–30, 134
Reid, Beth Heiden, 113, 119
REM sleep, 12
result-oriented thinking, 77
Rice University, 138–39
Roosevelt, Eleanor, 10, 153
Ryder Cup, 48–49

Salk, Jonas, 4–5, 25–26
San Diego Chargers, 92
San Francisco 49ers, 147–49
Sanskrit, 132
Santana, 103
self-actualization, 10–11, 24,
    29–30, 88
self-confidence. *See* confidence
self-doubt, 7
self-efficacy, 136
    see also confidence
selfishness, 113–14
self-love, 113–14
self-parody, 150
shared electrons, concept of, 4
Shea, Jack, 93–95
Shea, Jimmy, 93–95, 101, 102, 121
Shea, Jimmy, Sr., 93
Skeleton (winter sport), 93, 121
Smith, Rick, 17
social persuasion, 137, 140–41, 142–43
solipsism, 39–43
    exercise in, 43–45
Spiegel, David, 141
spiritual practices, 90
split-mind trance ability, 72–74, 75
Stanford University, 32, 136, 139–40,
    141
Stankowski, Paul, 137
Steiner, Oliver, 145
Stratton, G., 51
stressing out, 52–53
Sun Tzu, 15, 16, 25, 133

superego, 9–10
Suzuki, Shunryu, 53, 99

Talks to the Teachers (lectures), 31
"A Theory of Human Motivation"
    (Maslow), 10
theory of relativity, 4
therapists, 87
therapy, 90
thermodynamics, 132
thoughts. *See* emotions and thoughts
thought substitution, 96–97
Tiger trance, 72–74, 103
Tour de France, 32, 33, 146
    Armstrong, Lance, 121, 125–27
    Motorola Team, 125
training, 24–26, 90
trance, 72–74, 103
trust. *See* effort and trust, balance between
two scorecards exercise, 79–82

UCLA, 131
United Nations General Assembly
    (Vancouver, British
    Columbia), 3
University of Chicago, 48
University of Texas, 141
U.S. Open Golf Championship, 96–97
U.S. Open Tennis Championship, 6
U.S. Professional Cycling
    Championship, 33

Valvano, Jimmy, 128–29, 134
verbal persuasion, 137, 143

vicarious learning, 136, 140, 142
vision, 6–7
visualization
    accordion metaphor for relaxation,
        99–100
    of anger embodied in image of
        holding hot coal, 95
    attentional shift, 97–99, 149
    of emotion or thought floating
        downstream on a leaf,
        93–95
    transferring into action, 62–63

Washington, Denzel, 24
will
    energy of, 32–34
    exercising, 34–38
    self-actualization, 29–30
    solipsism, 39–45
    transforming desire into, tools for,
        38–39
Williamson, Marianne, 121
Wimbledon, 6
Wooden, John, 65
Woods, Tiger
    Beem's victory over, 137–38
    preshot routine of, 49
    putting practice, 65–66
    Tiger trance, 72–74, 103
    Zone-enhancing skills of,
        66–67

Zen, 53, 67, 99
Zen Mind, Beginner's Mind (Suzuki), 53

Michael Lardon, M.D., is a sports psychiatrist who has worked with many well-known PGA, NFL, and Olympic athletes. He is often interviewed by various national media, including CNN, *Sport Illustrated Magazine*, and *USA Today.* He is currently an Associate Clinical Professor of Psychiatry at the University of California San Diego. Visit his website at www.drlardon.com or www.knowmindsports.com.